Breaking Free

Breaking Free

SAIRA BRONSON

metro

Published by Metro Publishing Ltd,
3, Bramber Court, 2 Bramber Road,
London W14 9PB, England

www.blake.co.uk

First published in Hardback in 2005

ISBN 1 84358 135 3

British Library Cataloguing-in-Publication Data:

A catalogue record for this book is available from the British Library.

Design by www.envydesign.co.uk

Printed in Great Britain by CPD, Wales

1 3 5 7 9 10 8 6 4 2

Papers used by Metro Publishing are natural, recyclable products made from wood grown
in sustainable forests. The manufacturing processes conform to the environmental regulations
of the country of origin.

Every attempt has been made to contact the relevant copyright-holders, but some were
unobtainable. We would be grateful if the appropriate people could contact us.

Picture reproduced by kind permission of Rachel Luckhurst.

I dedicate this to my little soldier my daughter Sami, she has been the biggest strength in my life. I would have died a long time age if I didn't have her. Thanks Sami, and thanks for encouraging me and making me lots of cups of tea during the writing of this book.

Secondly to the memory of my father Aftab Uddin Ahmed, who dared to live all his life as a true warrior. I miss you dad. Please forgive me for not being there with you to say a final goodbye. But I know you are always with me.

Thirdly to my mother, mum you are the best mum in the world and I love you the most. I'm coming to see you soon, if you can wait fifteen years then another few years is nothing. Don't give up on me mum.

Finally to all the readers of my autobiography, don't settle for dreams, go on and achieve it, it's waiting for you. Don't look back.

ACKNOWLEDGEMENTS

First of all I'd like to thank my daughter Sami, I don't know what I'd have done without you Sami.

Secondly, thanks to my publisher John Blake and in particular, the senior editor James, for putting up with me during the editing of this book!

I'd also like to thank the social services in Newcastle, for protecting my daughter and helping me when I had nothing and nobody to turn to. You played a big part in my life and made my daughter's and my life a lot easier. Especially social worker Lisa Brazier. Also I'd like to thank Mandy Lambert from Newcastle Civic centre. And not to forget David Gray from David Gray solicitors in Newcastle.

Thanks to my friend, journalist Barney Snow from BBC television, Dipa Shah and Jill Martin from the *Mail* newspaper.

A special thanks to Governor Wolsey from Woodhill prison in Milton Keynes. You are a nice person, so stay nice.

I'd also like to say thanks to my solicitors, Picton Solicitors in Luton.

Thanks also to my friend Rachel Luckhurst, you are the best photographer and you know it.

A big thanks goes to Tariq and the staff from the Ethnic Minority Training Project in Luton.

I must also thank Hiron John, a 5th Dan Black Belt in Tae Kwondo from the UKTI/ILT Association. I have total respect for him, he is a true martial artist.

There is one last person I'd like to thank, and he is a television actor from India called Aakashdeep Saigal. He has inspired and empowered me in a very strange way, through the painful separation from Charlie. I think we get inspiration and empowerment from all sorts of people all the time, even from a small child. But all I know that when I was left in a deep dark corner to die an emotional death, Aakashdeep Saigal was the only light apart from my daughter Sami. Truthfully speaking, at that time I thought my life wasn't worth living, but thanks to my daughter and this actor, I'm alive and 100% hopeful towards my future again.

CONTENTS

1 PARADISE LOST

When I look back at my last 30 years of life, I see a lost soul crying for love. Too many deep wounds refuse to heal. The pain just won't fade away, leaving permanent scars that cut deep into my heart and soul. And the heartache never stops. I've given unconditionally to make others smile, but nobody listens to my soundless screams. Those who were dearest to me have stolen joy and laughter from me again and again, yet I've never turned my back on them; I've always been the backbone of their lives. At times, I'm afraid to reach out, as I know there would be nothing but darkness. It has been a lifetime's uphill struggle, but I have managed to rise above it all, and retain my pride and dignity. I must go on ... tomorrow is another day.

I'm an unlucky daughter who was unable to see her father when he died. I'm that same helpless sister who couldn't give her nine-year-old little brother the toy car that he wanted. I'm the same child who hasn't had the opportunity to hug her mother for the last 14 years. And it's been 14 years since I last saw my homeland.

At times of despair, I listen to the song 'I believe I can fly' by the American singer R Kelly again and again. For some reason, it encourages me to be strong:

I'm a Bangladeshi woman, come from a Muslim family, who was born and brought up in Bangladesh. I was born 1 June 1970. I was named Fatema when I was born, but I later changed my name to Saira. I spent my childhood on the tea estate where my father worked. The tea estates are among some of the most beautiful places in Bangladesh. They're like a paradise, with swathes of beautiful tea plants surrounded by mountains, on top of which are small houses. Jungle flowers grow everywhere, and small lakes lie like jewels around the lower slopes of the mountains as a perfect finishing touch, to complete the sense of supreme artistry. There is some sort of special connection between the jungle and me; I could live there quite happily all alone.

I was very young, but I can remember every detail of the tea estate where we lived quite clearly. It was very peaceful although lonely as well. None of our other relatives lived there, they lived far away in cities. Us children all had a good relationship with our parents even though my father was often away working. For some reason I remember spending more time with my father than with my brothers. They were always busy with their studies and friends. My parents were definitely more strict with my brothers than with me. Maybe because I was so young.

As a tea-estate manager my father's main duties were to go from area to area and inspect and supervise as well as managing factory workers. The factories made tea powder from the tea-tree leaves.

At night, I used to sit by the window to watch the moonlight gently dusting the tea plants. Sometimes, I used to feel as though somebody was calling me by name far away from the deep jungle.

My father was the senior forest officer for the estate; he earned a great deal of money. I would say that we were one of the richest families in the area. We only had a small family – my parents, my two elder brothers and myself. But we had a house full of servants for each household chore. I had my very own babysitter as well.

No doubt, I was the most loved child by everyone. We had everything we could ever want, except something that didn't make sense to me – my brothers and I weren't allowed to mix that much with the local kids. They were poor, and were believed to be 'lower caste'; not even our housekeepers were allowed to sit on the same chairs as us, even having to eat their dinner from different plates. They were also allocated a separate servants' quarters.

This system of segregation still exists in certain parts of Bangladesh. I never understood such nonsense as a child; I was so brainwashed that I used to believe that these poor 'lower caste' people were a sort of bad omen for us normal people. They were only our servants, after all! Obviously, when I was a little bit older, I realised that it was these people who had hearts of gold. Their only distinguishing features were those that society and the injustice of the class system had placed upon them. In all other respects, we were all the same at heart.

As part of the daily routine, my brothers – Jalal (the eldest) and Raj (the middle child) – would come home from school, then, after having dinner, have some rest and then get ready for Islamic classes. I would just sit there and watch them getting told off by the Muslim cleric. I never really concentrated on the religious studies, as I knew that soon we would move to the city, so I could go to school.

By the time I was six, my father took early retirement and we all moved to a city called Hobigonj. It was difficult for me to leave the comfort of the tea estate behind, as I was very attached to the lifestyle there and I missed the nature and the jungle, but I was also eager to make the most of the opportunities that now lay in store for me.

I soon adapted to city life and gradually allowed our childhood paradise to recede into a distant memory. But I was not immune to the usual childhood anxieties. On my first day at school, I would not let my father leave me. For some strange reason, I thought my father might not come to pick me up again. So, with my teacher's agreement, my father was allowed to stay in the room next to our classroom, and I only came out of lessons five times in two hours to see if he was still there! I'm glad to say that I didn't need my father with me at school any more after that, going on to enjoy my life at school enormously, and I would say I was very good at my studies.

A few months later, my mum told me that I was going to have a little brother or sister. We were all very happy, especially me. I was very excited because I always wanted a little brother or sister to play with. I had a good relationship with my older brother Jalal, although I didn't get on quite so well with Raj, but he knows I love him. I was still very close to my dad but I didn't enjoy the same relationship with my mother, as she was very strict with me. Much of this was probably because she believed, like most Bangladeshi mothers, that because I was a girl I might get out of control, and when I was older I might get into trouble and give the family a bad name.

Finally, the day came. When my baby brother, Joynal, was born, I was very happy. He was a really cute little baby … and still is! I felt really proud of him, and was delighted to have a little brother, so much so that I used to show him off to my friends.

Everything seemed to be going well for us, but all good things come to an end. I must have been at least 11 years old when I realised my life was becoming even more controlled, with even stricter rules and regulations – the carefree days of my early childhood had gone for good.

I had to stop wearing short, revealing clothing; I could only wear full-length clothes, which would cover my body entirely. I wasn't allowed to play outside that much or play with boys my own age. I can understand that, as my parents only wanted to protect me, but my family could have dealt with the situation in a loving, understanding way, rather than by being strict or imposing a harsh regime. They even beat me at times when I didn't want to listen to their inflexible demands and instructions. They never really let me grow or make my own mistakes, something I saw happening with many other 'ordinary' 11-year-olds.

The only time I used to have fun was when I was at school, after which I would come home, have something to eat then play with my little brother. I'd then go to the mosque for Islamic study. I hated the Muslim cleric there! During lessons, whenever I made a mistake he used to beat me really hard on my hands and face like a madman. I'm sure many Muslims can relate to this, as it's a common problem young people face when they take part in religious studies. When those lessons finished, I'd have to help my mother with the housework. Occasionally, I was allowed to go to my friend's house to play. That was my daily routine.

It may be difficult to believe, but I never told my mother when I started my period. I kept that a secret. I feared that, when she found out, my life would become stricter, or they might even try to get me married off! I managed to keep it a secret for two years, then, one day, my mother found out when I was suffering badly with period pain.

It is strange how everyone's behaviour towards me changed after that. I was constantly reminded how to behave like a grown-up, responsible woman. It felt as though, within a day, there were baskets full of responsibility dumped on my tiny shoulders! My worst fears had been confirmed – in their eyes, I had become a young adult over night.

There were so many things I wanted to learn, and so much I wanted to be part of, just like all my other friends. For example, I wanted to learn a classical dance called Kathak. Obviously, I wasn't allowed to. Wanting to learn dance or music isn't really acceptable in some Muslim families. My family thought that it was a degrading activity for a young Muslim girl. But that never stopped me dancing at home whenever my family was out. I used to put the music on and dance away, copying all the film actresses, while I made my little brother sit and watch the gate outside in case my parents came back.

Classical dance and music are my first love; they are my passion, my comfort; I can't survive without them. I think they're a form of gift from God, or else how could they have such a magical effect on us?

At the age of 13, I was in high school, my brothers were in college and my little brother started school himself. I was doing very well at my studies, and I'd managed to attract a boyfriend as well, whom I'd only meet during school time. I can't even remember his name now, but I do remember is that he was shorter than me! And I kept him a closely guarded secret from my family.

Eventually, though, my family did find out about him. They told his family to keep away from me. Just to avoid any problem from both of our families, we stayed away from each other.

2 TROUBLED TEENS

In many respects, I was like any other 14-year-old, but my home life was far from 'normal'. I had to accept and respect the beliefs of the rest of my family, and there was very little I could do to change their way of viewing the world. I also had to consider 'society' as well; it may be possible to change one person's attitude or belief, but not an entire society's.

I often got into trouble. I never seemed to fit in. I never enjoyed going to the mosque for religious studies. Often I used to lie to my mother that I'd been to the mosque, when really I'd just sit alone outside it while the lessons went on inside. Anything to avoid the lessons and the cleric's beatings. I always had tried to stay out to avoid my mother. For some reason I thought that she hated me and that was why she was strict with me. I had to think twice before I spoke, in case I said the wrong thing and got a slap across my face, or received a punishment from my mother or one of my older brothers.

No matter what I did, I was always in the wrong according to my mother. I must admit, though, that my father sometimes defended me, or tried to encourage my mother to be less strict towards me. But that never worked; instead, they would both end up arguing over me, and then there would be an awful atmosphere.

I've always been close to my father; he loved me the most. My father was one of the most intelligent men I have ever known. He was a very highly educated person. Before he married my mother, he used to be a headmaster of a high school, while also being heavily involved in politics. He was well respected and praised by many people from different parts of Bangladesh. My father was a man of great stature to many people in Bangladesh and will always be a legend in my eyes. I remember he used to tell me that you could have your dreams and ambitions, but you sometimes have to compromise so that you don't hurt any of your loved ones. You also had to consider the society that you live in. And he told us regularly that education was the most important key to independence.

At the age of 14, I knew that my life was fast becoming a complete disaster. While I was still at school, the marriage proposals started to arrive for me. Some of my relatives weren't helping matters either. They would influence my parents by saying things like 'The sooner your daughter gets married, the better'… 'These days, you can't really trust young girls' … 'You never know what they might get up to at school or college' … and so on.

I begged my parents not to listen to anyone, and resist having me married off. My father and my brother Jalal were the only two people who understood, but my mother and some of our close relatives looked at the situation differently. They all believed that, because I was a girl, I didn't need any further education, and that marriage was the final destination in a woman's life anyway. My mother used to say that, by going to school or college, one day I might run off with a man and bring shame to the family. What she really meant was that she didn't trust me.

You can imagine how helpless and frightened I felt, as I tried everything in my power to avoid them marrying me off. I did succeed for a while but, as a result of that, I was seen as an ungrateful, disobedient daughter in everyone's eyes. The family and our relatives disliked me so much, which was really hurtful, because there is nothing worse than your own family turning against you, ignoring you or showing no love towards you. I felt like an outsider in my own house, often feeling extremely lonely and ended up crying alone. Loneliness became my best friend.

It was around this time that I became aware of, and then inspired by, a really special person. She was from India, where she is known as the 'bandit queen', but her real name is Phoolan Devi. She will always remain my inspiration in life, in terms of how she stood up to and overcame the utmost hardship. She is my hero.

Unfortunately, I never met Phoolan Devi but I read a great deal about how she fought for her beliefs against a group of evil men in our society. She was victimised by a group of upper-caste men for being lower caste. Her parents got her married off when she was only 11, and her husband was the first of many rapists in her life. Then, later on, she was gang-raped by upper-caste so-called community leaders.

She continued to battle and tried to survive at the same time, becoming notorious in her struggles and eventually joined a gang of bandits. During this period in her life, she was charged with robbery and, while she was in police custody, she was beaten and raped by police officers. So Phoolan Devi became a fully fledged bandit, took the law into her own hands and ended up killing some upper-caste men who had raped her. She was then captured and sent to prison. On her release from prison in 1995, a female majority elected her to Parliament. A few years later, she was brutally killed in front of her own house.

I think most women would respect everything she stood for. I gained a lot of confidence from Devi, and, if I would ever have had the chance, I would have kissed her shoes for being my strength throughout my life. I strongly believe there is a Devi inside most

Asian women, and that it only comes out when people push us to the limit.

What an evil world we live in. Why take something away from a woman by force, when it can be achieved by love? All my heartfelt love and respect to Devi – she will always be my inspiration and strength.

Because of my increasingly unacceptable behaviour at home, one of my aunts one day advised my mother to take me to a 'black magic' holy man. Maybe he could do something to make me listen to my parents and be a perfect daughter! That went on for quite a while. Eventually, I had no choice but to go with my mother; the alternative was to suffer a beating from my mother and my brother Raj.

I used to hate going to that place. I would be given 'holy water' to drink and plenty of free advice – how to be a good girl, pray all the time, cover up my body from head to toe, listen to my parents, otherwise I'd go to burning hell when I die.

I used to think, 'How can he say that? How does he know what God is thinking?' This is the same 'holy' man who nearly killed me once by feeding me dirty, infected 'holy' potions. As I became very ill, our doctor realised that it could only have been the 'holy' medicines that must have caused the infection. Although my father and older brother Jalal stood by me, and tried to stop these unnecessary – and potentially life-threatening – visits, they couldn't do much to help me because it's part of our culture that generally mothers are given almost total control of their daughters.

My father, at that time, had other things to concentrate on as well. The farm my father set up wasn't doing too well, and we were struggling financially. On top of that, my brother Raj was mixing with a bad crowd which was causing increasing tension at home. As a result, my mother developed depression as well. The only positive event in our lives at that time was that my older brother found a good job outside the city soon after graduating from college.

In everyone's mind, the cause of the greatest tension in our household was my prospective marriage. I was made to feel like a massive burden on my parents' shoulders and they wanted to be free of that burden as soon as possible. My father used to have long conversations with me sometimes, trying his best to make me understand in a very loving way why he wanted me to get married as soon as I was 16. Often, he used to tell me that he was getting old and it was a big responsibility to leave behind. He wanted to see me happily married to someone, as I was his only daughter … and maybe he had a point.

So, within a few weeks, I was stopped from going to school. Everyone kept on saying it was for the best. I don't think I can express just how much I missed my school and all my friends. In the morning, I used to watch my friends going to school, and look at my school uniform and cry silently. I often had dreams at night in which I was all ready to go to school. I was also in my final year; one more year and then I would have been able to go to college. My life was full of tears at that time, and all I could see ahead of me was darkness.

One of our relatives in particular had a lot of influence over my family at that time. I went to him for help, and he reassured me that he would make my family change their minds on the school matter. I felt so relieved.

So the next day, with my parents' permission, I went to this relation's house, as I wasn't going to let it go without a fight. I stayed in his house for two days and had a good time with his family. On the third day, my relative said it was all good news, but we had to talk later in private.

I was delighted that I could finally go to college and didn't have to get married. Later that night, after dinner, his wife and son went to sleep; it must have been around 10.00pm, and we were talking. First, I told him how much I appreciated his help; he just held my hand and said he would do anything for me.

At first, I thought he was just being kind to me, then, as I pulled my hands away, he wouldn't let them go. I felt very uncomfortable as he started pulling me towards him. I kept on saying, 'Please let me go ... I want to leave now!' But he didn't listen to anything I said.

'If you make me happy, I'll not hurt you,' he said, 'and don't even think of shouting because you know very well how embarrassing it will be for you! I'm a man ... nothing will happen to me. People would only shame you!'

I was crying without making a noise, and felt so frightened that I started to shake like a leaf. I simply didn't know what to do. That bastard was touching me and frightening me, saying, 'Don't even think about shouting, because if people find out then, in the future, nobody will ever marry you.'

I suddenly became really angry then, and tried to push him away, whereupon he slapped me hard on my face. Then he started to pull my hair very hard and, before I knew it, he'd punched me on my breast. As I was still struggling to get away from him, I started to shout out for his wife to come down. Thank God she heard me and soon rushed into the room. Her husband then said that I was upset because my parents wouldn't let me go to school and he was just trying to calm me down.

I came home that night and didn't say a word about that to anybody. My entire body was in pain, and my left breast where he'd punched me was so painful that it had swollen up. I then had a temperature for a few days after that as well.

I thought to myself, 'Why did he do that to me? What did I do to deserve that? What can I do about this? Who do I go to?' I couldn't even tell my family anything, as I felt too embarrassed to talk about that animal. I just kept on turning things over in my mind, but couldn't come up with any solution. I tried to forget about the whole awful experience, but it's very difficult to forget about

something as traumatic as that. It leaves you with a deep, long-
lasting scar, for which the only remedy seems to be the love and
consideration of a genuinely good person – nothing else.

What added to my pain was the fact that he kept coming to our
house as normal, mixing with my family as though nothing had
happened. I even had to make him cups of tea as usual, something
my mother made me do for any guest who came to our house. I
hated doing that for him so much that, one day, I put lots of chilli
powder in his tea, hoping he would choke on it! And it worked! His
eyes nearly popped out. I gave him some water after that as I didn't
want that pig of a man to die on my doorstep. After that, he avoided
drinking tea in our house again, especially when I made it.

I had finally realised that I should forget about further education
at college. My family and relatives eventually decided that they
would marry me off in a couple of years, as soon as an acceptable
proposal came along. I was told that in that two years I should learn
how to do the housework, pray regularly and learn to be responsible,
as all of these qualities are essential in a wife. From that moment on,
I knew very well that, no matter what I did, I wouldn't be able to stop
myself being crucified in the name of culture and religion.

Every few months, I had to face marriage proposals. They were
all presented through a middle-man, a sort of broker. He would tell
my family all the details regarding the suitor's background and
current status, and then, if my family liked what they heard, they
would invite the man and his family to our house.

Whenever these visits occurred, I'd have to dress up nicely and sit
in front of them. After some small-talk and refreshments, they
would start asking me questions, such as 'What's your name?' and
'Can you cook?' All the while, I wasn't allowed to talk unless I was
spoken to directly, as it was considered rude. On one occasion, one
man's mother asked me to walk up and down the room to make
sure that I didn't have any disability! On another occasion, a suitor's

sister-in-law pulled my hair to check that it was real and not a wig! After these initial introductions, I'd have to leave the room and let the others do all the talking.

If things went well, my family would be invited back to their house to talk about matters further. The slight difference here is that my family didn't get to do any hair-pulling or make the man parade in front of them! They only sat and talked, or went out somewhere. It's a much more relaxed affair visiting the man's home and family. What double standards! Then, of course, if both parties are happy with everything, the marriage planning takes place.

What could I do? I couldn't run away; even if I did, where would I go? In Bangladesh at that time, we didn't have any facilities like in the UK, such as women's refuges, women's aid or support groups. But I just couldn't give up on life without a struggle. I couldn't run away, though, as I would only have brought shame on my family. Most of all, I didn't want to hurt my father.

My education and my friends were the only two things I had and, when they were taken away from me, the anger started to well up inside me. I just wanted to escape from everything. Some days I wouldn't eat or speak to anyone; I'd just go to bed and break down in tears. Some nights, I would cry and cry until I fell asleep.

Often, I used to have a very strange dream; there would be a man in it, comforting me. The weirdest part was that I could never remember his face in the morning. I often used to have that dream, although it would remain mystifying and unexplained. It's strange how something as inexplicable as that inspired me to wake up in the morning with a smile on my face.

It seemed that I had no escape route, although there was always the final option – suicide. So one day, I tried to do just that.

That morning, when I woke up, I felt as though there was no point in staying alive. We had some sort of insecticide in the house, so I simply poured about a cupful down my throat. Straight away, my throat burned like hell; I didn't know what was happening to me. Everything became dark all around me. I felt as though that was it – I was dying. I just wanted my father. I shouted out for him to come and hold me. He wasn't in the house at that time as he'd gone out for his regular morning walk. Obviously, by then, everyone else in the house realised what I had done.

My mother rushed to me; a few neighbours had come along as well. I was crying as my throat was killing me. One of the neighbours put her finger in my mouth to make me vomit. That didn't work; instead, she ended up scarring my mouth with her nails. Then, to make things worse, one of the other neighbours said to my mother that the only way to save me was to force cow dung down my throat; that would make me throw up and, hopefully, the poison would come out.

Within half-an-hour, somebody got some cow dung from the nearest farm. They mixed that with some water and told me to drink it. I shook my head, telling them that I wouldn't drink it, crying at the same time for my father. But, before I knew it, four to five women held me tight and poured it down my throat. I vomited immediately, and I begged them not to force me to have any more, but they wouldn't listen to me. Then I must have fallen unconscious.

A little while later, I found myself in hospital. I knew I was in the right place; I wanted to live. But my treatment hadn't finished yet. I had no idea that the hospital would put me through a near-death experience, as they decided to pump my stomach.

The nurses took me to a room; first, they put a mouth guard on me in order to allow access for a pipe through my mouth and into my stomach. Obviously, the Health Service in a small Bangladeshi town wasn't sufficiently well-equipped to provide an anaesthetic throat spray to numb my throat to avoid hurting me any further. So they just shoved that pipe into my mouth and pushed it as far down as they could.

My throat was already burning before the treatment, and now the pipe was slowly killing me, while two nurses held both of my hands, and two others held my feet. I couldn't move. Then one nurse poured some salt water down the pipe. Then, after a few minutes when my stomach was full, they removed the mouth guard so I could throw up.

This painful procedure was repeated three times. After that, I just couldn't breathe properly; I felt as though my eyes were popping out. I was very close to death, never having felt so much pain in my entire life. I tried to tell them that I couldn't breathe, but I couldn't communicate properly because of the mouth guard. I tried struggling physically as well, to make the nurses let go of me, so I could tell them that I had difficulty breathing. But they refused to listen to me; one of the nurses even said to me in a very angry voice, 'We are trying to save your life, so you should be grateful to us!' Somewhere in the corner of the room, I saw my parents standing. They were worried but also trying to cover their faces in shame about the whole thing. I just wanted them both to come to me, hold me and say that everything was going to be all right.

Do you know what the most humiliating part was? The room where they were giving me the treatment was open to public view from various points, so everyone in the general area gathered round to see what was going on. They all looked through the two big open windows, desperately wanting to see the girl who had tried to commit suicide. Can you begin to imagine how humiliated I felt? At that moment, I wished I'd died instead of being humiliated like that in public!

By the time they finished working on me, I couldn't remember a thing; I must have lapsed into unconsciousness again, I suppose. I don't know if I had a dream or some sort of hallucination, but for a few minutes I felt as though a man was gently helping me to get up from where I was lying. Then he led me to a room full of flowers, which didn't look like a hospital room, where there was a profound feeling of peace and quiet. He held my hand and told me, 'It's not your time to go yet … you have a long way to go.'

I can remember very clearly how he looked and what he was wearing, even in the condition that I was in. He had the most distinctive brown eyes, shoulder length-curly hair and stubble on his face. He was wearing a black dhooti (a lovely loincloth worn by mainly Hindu men in Asia, particularly in Bangladesh and India). He then held me very gently and close to him. As I was just about to close my eyes, I heard a knock at the door.

I immediately woke up, and found myself in another room of the hospital. My family was next to me. I tried to recall the nature of the dream, but I couldn't concentrate clearly. I wanted to talk but couldn't get the words out of my mouth; all I could feel was the pain in my stomach and my burning throat, and I felt very weak. My father was saying to me, 'You are in safe place … everything will be all right now.' I was given strong painkillers, and fell asleep again.

I had to stay in the hospital for two days, then I came back home. After that incident, my family was a little bit more considerate towards me, but at the same time they were angry with me for having attempted something so drastic.

After I was discharged from hospital, the local people – mainly the youngsters – made my life hell. They used to torment me about my suicide attempt. To them, it was a golden opportunity to tease me and to spread all sorts of gossip about me trying to kill myself.

How could they poke fun at someone desperate enough to have tried to commit suicide? I couldn't believe it, and was sickened by it. In retrospect, I can understand to some extent why they behaved as they did; my experience is that, if a young Asian girl tries to or commits suicide, people automatically look down on her, rather than try to understand the reasons for her actions. I just had to remain a mute spectator while people assassinated my character.

A few weeks later, my mother's older brother, Shahid Miah, and his family came to visit us. We used to call him 'Big Uncle' because he is physically large and is the eldest in the family. Everyone respected and listened to him, including my father. While he was with us, he suggested to my mother that it would be good for everyone if I went back to stay with them in their house for a few months, as it would give everyone a break. At the same time, it might allow enough time for people in the neighbourhood to forget about the suicide attempt.

My father allowed me to go. I was very happy because my cousins were the same age as me, and it meant I'd be staying in Dhaka, the capital city of Bangladesh, and I was looking forward to seeing it.

A few days later, I left with them, and was made to feel really welcome when we arrived. My uncle is a very rich and influential man, and is highly regarded, and so I grabbed the opportunity to savour a quite different and exciting lifestyle.

I loved living in their house but missed my own home as well, particularly my father and my little brother Joynal. I must admit I felt left out seeing all my cousins going to college, but I was happy there. I even made a friend. His name was Iddriss, and he used to go to college with one of my cousins and lived opposite my uncle's house. He would come up to my window and we would talk and laugh for ages. We only ever met up by the front window whenever no one was around. I used to be inside the house and Iddriss used to stand outside. There were bars going across the window, so we used to hold hands through them while we talked.

We grew to like each other a lot. I don't know if that was love or not, but we certainly got on really well. He made me feel happy and valued as a human being. It was the way he used to look at me, and I like a man who can look at me like that – almost looking *through* me and reading me like a book. It's then that a man can touch you deep inside, as though you're an extension of his own body.

I know he certainly had a lot of affection for me. But my uncle's family didn't approve of our friendship, as young men and women weren't allowed to mix like that. But I knew what that was all about; it all went back to the fact that none of my family trusted me at all.

Dhaka is a beautiful city; I loved living there, and I was very happy in my uncle's house. Everyone was very friendly towards me. People in Dhaka seemed a lot more open-minded than in Hobigonj, my home city. I stayed in their house for about six months, but then my family started to insist that I return home.

So my older brother was duly dispatched to collect me. Of all the people I would miss, there was one whose friendship meant a great deal to me – Iddriss. The day I left, I called Iddriss over and said that I was going home that evening. His smile just melted away; he couldn't believe it. He just looked at me, not knowing what to do or say. He knew that he would never see me again. He just stroked my face through the window and said that everything would be all right and that he'd never forget me. His eyes welled up; I knew he wanted to say more, but he couldn't. I was lucky to have found a friend like him.

Later that evening, I left my uncle's house with my brother for the station. We had to wait a while for the train, so we went to a coffee shop. As I looked outside, I saw Iddriss frantically searching for me in the crowd, but he couldn't see me. That was the first time I'd ever experienced someone liking me so much that he had to try to find me. But there was very little I could do; I couldn't shout to Iddriss as I was with my older brother. So I consoled myself with the thought that, if Iddriss really loved me, he would come and look for me, and that one day he would find me.

Finally, it was time for us to leave and, as my brother and I sat on the train, it was only then that Iddriss noticed me. He stood there as the train slowly started to gather speed away from the platform, and away from Iddriss. Soon, I couldn't see him, and I felt really sad. But, by then, I was becoming used to everything being snatched away from me. That was the last time I saw Iddriss.

I was really happy to be back in my own house, though; no matter what my family had done to me, I never had any less love for them. Most of all, I missed my little baby brother. In a few days, I couldn't help noticing that my father seemed very different and detached from everything. I was worried and sat down to talk to him about it. He told me that my brother Raj had become very difficult to deal with; he wouldn't find a job and all his friends were troublemakers, who were regularly leading him astray. My father added that Raj sometimes even became aggressive towards him for not giving him money.

I just couldn't believe it. For some reason, Raj believed that our father didn't love him enough, and that he hadn't helped him enough in finding a career. He and my father regularly had arguments, and months would go by without them speaking to each other.

I could see why my father was worried and angry with him. We just couldn't understand why he was like that. I tried to talk to Raj, but that didn't work either, as he never really took any interest in what I had to say. Slowly, things went from bad to worse.

One evening, as usual, he came home and started to argue with my father about not being given an amount of money he needed for some business. Things got out of hand that evening and Raj became violent. I had the shock of my life that day. I just couldn't believe it. How on earth could anybody hit a defenceless 70-year-old man?

There were similar occurrences after that and, when my mother and I tried to stop Raj, I even got hit a few times, as he used to become very angry.

At the same time, we all knew that Raj wasn't really aware of what he was doing. He was very confused and quite ill around that time. I felt sorry for him sometimes, as he seemed like a lost soul.

He didn't really have any direction in life, and he'd become very unpredictable, listening to all sorts of people and getting into trouble. He also seemed quite ill physically most of the time.

I used to feel quite useless; I wanted to do something to help him, but all I could do was to pray to God. I can still remember my regular prayer: 'Give me all the sadness but, in return, keep everyone in my family well and happy.'

Finally, my father managed to find Raj a job through one of his associates, whom we used to call 'Judge Uncle', a judge in the Supreme Court in Dhaka. This 'uncle' had been one of my father's students while my father was headmaster at the high school in his early days.

It was interesting how most of the students kept in touch with my father, even after many years. Whenever they came to our house, they never used to call my father by his name, they always called him 'Sir', even in front of their children. It's all to do with respect; in our culture, we have great respect for teachers, and in some areas you don't even look a teacher in the eye, as it could be considered rude.

Fortunately, Judge Uncle had found Raj a job in an engineering company, where he would be provided with training as well. My father was relieved that at least he had secured some sort of job and, best of all, Judge Uncle said that Raj could stay with him and his family in their house. That way, he could keep an eye on him. My brother was happy and accepted the job, and we were all happy for him.

Thank God that, after Raj found a job, the atmosphere at home became a little bit better. As far as my own situation was concerned, I think I had learned to accept my life as it was. My day-to-day existence only revolved around doing the housework, helping my mother with cooking and looking after my little brother, Joynal, which I really enjoyed.

Because my mother suffered from depression, I ended up looking after my little brother most of the time. I was more of a mother to him than a sister. I don't really blame my mother – it wasn't her fault that she was depressed. I think that was all brought on by her worry. I tried to be as helpful as I could be but, whenever she was in a bad mood, she used to take her anger out on me by shouting at me then beating the hell out of me, even over a little mistake. But I never held it against her or hated her; we didn't have a good relationship then, but she knew that I loved her deeply. You only get one mother; I still love her, no matter what she did to me.

Just as everything was going fine, my father's farming business started to experience some serious problems. Unfortunately, a few of the managers of the business took advantage of my father's kind nature. Basically, we were left struggling financially; we had to survive on very little, but we did manage somehow.

From my viewpoint, I couldn't see any answers to our problems. From being one of the richest families in Bangladesh, we had become one of the poorest. But, because of the way we had been brought up, the finances never mattered to us. Our values were too strong to let that matter to us. On top of all that, Raj's contract finished, so he left his job and came back home. I thought then that my father and Raj would inevitably end up fighting again.

With my own eyes, I witnessed my family starting to fall apart, and there was nothing I could do. One particular incident I'll remember for the rest of my life. My little baby brother Joynal, after coming back from school one day, said to my mother, 'I'm fed up eating only one type of vegetable week after week, can we have a chicken curry, please?' When I heard that, I was heartbroken. I felt completely helpless. My baby brother wanted to have a chicken curry and I was unable to give him it. I felt ashamed of myself, as up to that point I had only really thought about my own situation.

I couldn't sleep that night with my brother's words going round and round in my head. And I knew that I had to do something. So, the next day, I sold my only pair of gold earrings, and bought the biggest chicken and some meat from the market for my baby brother. Well, that's what he wanted, and that's exactly what he would get!

When my father saw what I had done, he felt so guilty that he broke down in tears; he felt as though he had lost the struggle to provide us with the best of everything. But I know he had done all he could for us, and tried to pull together the remains of the family business. Even in that desperate situation, he bought my little brother and me new clothes for festivals and celebrations, while he wore the only shirt and pair of trousers he had with pride.

I had never met anyone to rival my father. What I find most amazing is that, since the age of 14, he had been his family's only provider. His parents were old and unable to work, and they came from a poor family. But my father decided to change his fate when only just into his teens. He walked three miles to his school; he borrowed books from his friends, as he couldn't afford to buy his own, and then, in the evenings, he offered private tuition to children, to earn money to look after his parents.

As far as I'm concerned, only a true legend could do something like that. Later on, he graduated from one of the top universities in Bangladesh, with degrees in subjects such as Politics, Teaching and Islamic Studies. After his graduation, he started teaching in a college, and at the same time he was heavily involved in politics. He was secretary to the Habigonj Subdivisional Muslim Students Federation Party. One of his friends and classmates was Abdussamad Azad, who was the foreign secretary of Bangladesh up to 2001. They studied together at Sylhet College in Bangladesh. I'm sure Mr Azad remembers my father very well. Then, after marrying my mother, he got the job at the tea estate. Yes, I'm proud of my father – he is a hero in my eyes.

It saddens me that, all things considered, I remained one of his main worries. He wanted me to be happily married before he died; he often used to say that to me. He'd also tell me that one of his dreams was to see me married to someone from England, because he believed I would be happy and I would never have to suffer at the hands of a cruel or selfish husband. England is known throughout the world as one of the 'civilised' countries and, like other gullible fathers from Bangladesh, my father believed that an English–Bangladeshi husband would guarantee a happy future.

When I went to bed at night, all I could do was to hide my face and cry. I knew my father was right and wanted the best for me, but I didn't know how to accept this new turn of events over my possible marriage to an Englishman.

It was around that time that one of our neighbours, called Ashiq, who was also my brother's friend, used to come to our house. Soon, we started to enjoy each other's company. Sometimes, I was allowed to go to his house, but my family didn't know at that time anything about us liking each other. A few months went by like that, and then Ashiq said to me one day that he loved me and wanted to marry me. I knew very well that my marriage was in the process of being fixed with a man from England, so I had to stop myself falling in love with Ashiq, let alone getting married to him.

So I made a decision there and then to put my own desires completely to one side and devote myself to my family, so I could make some sort of difference. To start with, I took over all the duties of our housekeeper. We had to let her go, because we didn't have sufficient to pay her salary. And when I say 'housework', it was a long way from what we understand housework to be in England. This was on a completely different scale and much harder.

For instance, I had to use a clay oven to cook in because we couldn't afford to have a gas or electric cooker. And we didn't have any running water in our house either, so I had to use our next-door neighbour's. I would have to take a bucket with me and fill that with water, and then walk back and forth at least ten times before I'd manage to fill our own big bucket, which we'd then keep in a cool area. I also did all the usual cleaning, and helped my mother with the cooking. I also did all our family washing by hand twice a week, which is why, when people shake my hand, they ask me why my hands are so rough. I just smile and say they are hard-working hands!

Last, but not least, the hardest job was still to be done – making the mixed spices for all our curries, meals and special occasions. I had to grind an entire row of spices on a flat piece of rock and turn them into fine powder. There was no machine to help with this, it was all done by hand, and sometimes both my hands used to burn like hell and bleed at the same time, particularly when I had to grind the hot chillies. My mother would help sometimes, but she couldn't help all the time, though, because she was by then a little too old for the really tough chores. But I never complained, even though, at times, it all seemed too much to bear.

3 VEIL OF TEARS

At that point in my life, marriage proposals were flooding in thick and fast from all directions. One particular proposal was sent to my father one day. A British Bangladeshi man came to Bangladesh to get himself a second wife (he already had one back in England). He had seen me at some wedding I'd been to, he liked me, and so he'd asked my father if he could have my hand. As part of the deal, he promised my father that I would have my own bank balance and a house in my name in Bangladesh. He expected my father to hand me over on the basis of the offer of a few material possessions. My father told him, 'My daughter is not for sale! I might be poor, but I still have my sanity left.'

I could not believe it; a man can't abuse his wife any worse than that! If I'd been his first wife, I would have cut his penis off, and then said, 'Now you can go and get married however many times you wish! You have my full permission!'

At around that time, my mother had a relative who was also constantly bringing marriage proposals. God, I used to hate him! I still do! Would you believe that idiot had two wives? And he used to flirt with anything that looked vaguely like a woman! Some women used to say how he had taken advantage of them by saying he would help them financially or he would get them a job on his farm. None of those women ever complained openly about him, though. Yes, I bet he served the community all right, by harassing young girls at night, perhaps! I find it difficult to understand who had voted for him to become a prominent figure. I wouldn't even have him clean my shoes, never mind give him such a responsible position.

So he started to turn up at our house a lot with marriage proposals. I hated the way he used to look at me, from head to toe, just like a third-class pervert! It was as though he knew he couldn't touch me, but he would let his dirty mind tick over with disgusting thoughts. It wasn't a look you can forget in a hurry.

Within a few weeks of this sort of treatment, the evil man found a husband for me, and managed to fool my family at the same time. He said that the man's family was very rich and that they lived in England. The man himself was apparently a very nice person, that he'd been born and brought up in England, but had good Asian cultural values. Obviously, he had come to Bangladesh with his mother to find a nice Bangladeshi girl and get married. So, basically, my mother's uncle did a very good job convincing my family to consider this proposal seriously … and he succeeded.

Well, I thought privately that I might as well start preparing myself for the worst nightmare of my life. Then, at the same time, I clung to the hope that my prospective husband might turn out to be the nice, caring man we had been told about, and that I might actually be worrying unnecessarily. Who knows, I might even fall in love with him … I just had to wait to find out and, anyway, what could I do but wait and see?

In a few more weeks, the wedding preparations started in our house, and the first main event was the groom's family coming to see me. That day, both of my brothers were there as well, and few of my close friends. Everyone was happy and lent a hand cleaning the entire house and cooking for our guests. In the evening, the groom's family arrived – there was the groom's mother, sister, older brother and his wife, as well as the man responsible for this possible marriage. The groom chose not to be present at this early meeting and sometimes a groom may not meet his bride until the day of the wedding ceremony itself.

My friends got me all ready in a nice sari and helped me with my make-up. Then, once they'd had dinner, my father came up to my room to take me to meet them. I walked into the room with my head down in a very feminine manner, as that's how a bride is supposed to look. My father introduced me to them; first, they asked my name and threw a few other questions at me, then the groom's sister took me to my room to talk to me in private, while the elders got on with the other wedding arrangements.

So there I was, sitting in my room with the groom's sister as she began to interview me. And that's exactly what it felt like, an interview. She asked me all kinds of questions – Can I cook? Did I have any boyfriends? Would I be able to live in England without my family?

At that point, the prospective mother-in-law joined us. She sat near me and took my hands in hers, which I thought was her way of trying to be nice. But, within a few seconds, I realised she was paying particular attention to my hands – she was checking to see whether I had ten fingers! Then she moved my veil from my head and thoroughly inspected my hair.

These were all the usual things I had been through during previous marriage proposals, and I was becoming very annoyed but kept quiet. Then the sister told me that her brother was very nice, and that he'd look after me. I actually looked at her and wanted to believe her. I didn't ask her any questions because it's traditional at that stage for the bride not to ask anything. Once the discussions were over, they left.

The next day, it was my family's turn to go to the groom's house to meet him, so I stayed at home during their visit. They came back after few hours, and they all had big smiles on their faces. I just knew it! I realised that everything had gone well and that there was no going back now.

Later on, my older brother Jalal wanted to discuss everything with me, so he made me a cup of tea and we sat down. We often did that whenever he was at home, as I was close to him. He told me all about the groom's family – the groom's name was Nunu, but his proper name was Muzibur Rehman. I just couldn't stop laughing when I heard the name Nunu! I said to my brother that, as he'd got a funny name, he'd probably look funny as well!

Jalal said he seemed a nice person and that his family didn't want a dowry from us. The dowry was something that the bride's family had to give to the groom and his family, an old tradition that has been practised in most parts of our culture for many years. The dowry could be anything from a new set of furniture for the house or some money to property in the groom's name. So I was relieved to hear that they didn't want a dowry.

I then told Jalal that I wanted to meet Nunu at least once, if I was allowed, to see if I liked him. After all, I was the one marrying him. He said he would talk to the rest of the family and see what happened.

Meanwhile, my father was desperately trying to get enough money together for the wedding because we were still struggling financially. And, soon afterwards, I was allowed to meet up with the groom, although the meeting had to take place at the house of my mother's. I couldn't believe it, but I had to go along with it because I didn't have any choice.

So there I was, sitting in this strange room, waiting for the groom to arrive. All the time, crazy thoughts surged through my mind. What if he is the one I've been waiting for? Is he the man of my dreams? This could turn out to be the happiest day of my life!

I was interrupted by a knock on the door, and in walked mother's relative. He was followed by the groom. I simply couldn't believe my bad luck! He *was* just as ugly as his name! I couldn't believe my eyes! I was in total shock. Then I thought to myself that he could actually be a really nice person, so I shouldn't immediately judge him on his appearance, but I was finding it very hard to convince myself. He was just so ugly!

The three of us sat down and he introduced himself; he then asked my name and which school I went to. That's all he wanted to know. I never asked him anything, as he didn't give me the chance. After talking at me for about 15 minutes, he left.

Eventually, mother's relative told me that the groom liked me! That was that – the arrangements for the engagement had started. I then asked my mother whether my opinion counted for anything. What about how I felt about him? I didn't even like the way he looked. My family reassured me that he was very nice person, and I would be well looked after. Even though he had been born and brought up in England, he was still highly cultured and religious.

I told my father directly that I didn't like him and that I still knew so little about him, begging him not to marry me off to him. He sat me down and put his arms around me. Then he said to me that a person's looks aren't everything; inside, he might be nicer than I gave him credit for. He said, 'We've looked into his background, and he's really nice and he would love you. He promised me that he would love you and look after you. I wouldn't let anyone treat you badly, not while I'm alive, anyway. You get married, then go to England; I promise you that you will find the happiness you are looking for.'

My father reminded me again that he was an old man, so before he died he wanted to see me happily married; only then could he die in peace. When he said that, I looked at him and I could see in his eyes that that was what he wanted more than anything. I said no more on the subject.

I wanted to run away somewhere, but I just couldn't do that when I thought of my father. That would have destroyed him. I've seen some instances when women have run away. Eventually, they are persuaded to come back by their families, but then nobody wants to marry them! Why? Because the woman might not be a virgin any more, or they must have had deficiencies in their character to have run away in the first place!

Can you believe this? Why all the fuss? Why not learn to accept them for the people they are? Why worry if she's a virgin or not, or if she had a previous boyfriend? And why do we allow such double standards to prevail? Why can't men be men and love a woman for her mind, body and soul? Does a women ever ask a man whether he is a virgin or not? Of course not! It's simply an outdated, irrelevant obsession some men have.

Of course, I'm not saying that there aren't some women who don't have any self-respect, and there are those who give women a bad name. Any normal man with basic common sense wouldn't look twice at them.

But, however I felt about my situation, there was very little I could do, so I decided to leave everything in destiny's hand ... and I prepared myself for the worst. A few weeks later, the first stage of that was set in motion – my engagement.

A few days before the engagement itself, partying started in our house. Everyone was happy except me. Lots of our relatives and friends came over to stay for my engagement, and then for the wedding. On the day of the engagement, in the evening, Nunu's family came to our house with the engagement ring. After dinner and all the socialising, it was time to exchange the engagement rings. I was sitting there already with all my friends; they had got me all dressed up in a bridal sari and make-up.

Everyone said how beautiful I looked and talked among themselves, but I didn't hear any of their conversation. It's hard to explain how I felt; I could have been sad, happy, angry ... or a combination of all three. I suppose I mostly felt numb. Soon, the ring exchange took place, and after that they all left the room, leaving me with my friends. Some of my friends said to me, 'You should be very happy ... he seems a very nice person ...' but I just kept quiet.

Within a few days, the wedding day was fixed. Then, soon afterwards, I heard my father talking to my mother, saying that we were short of money for the wedding, and that he felt that he should give a small amount of household furniture as a dowry. People would talk, otherwise, and he didn't want anyone to point their finger at me because my father hadn't been able to afford a dowry. My poor father didn't know what to do, he was so worried; night after night, I watched him sitting outside turning things over in his mind.

My father tried to sell some of our land in the village, but at that time of the year nobody wanted to buy any land. So my father placed an advertisement to sell the open space in front of our house, as there was a little bit of unused land.

Some of that windfall went towards the wedding expenses, and my father used the rest of the money to buy some brand-new furniture as a gift for the groom. He also bought new clothes as a gift for the groom's family, and a gold wedding ring and some new suits for the groom.

With only three days to go before the wedding day, the whole house was full of relatives and family and everyone was busy decorating the house and having fun. Well, that's the whole point of any wedding – fun. The henna ceremony was celebrated on the next night; it's the part of the wedding ceremony in which henna patterns are applied to the bride's hands. Usually, it's an event only the women attend. My entire female friends and female relatives got together to paint my hands with henna, while we played loud music and generally had a really good time.

I was sitting there in a red sari, and my hair was decorated with yellow flowers. Two of my friends were doing the henna decorating, while others were dancing and having fun. I think the only man allowed in there was the one making the video. But, however beautiful it may have appeared on the surface, it's only truly beautiful when the bride is happy as well.

The party went on 'til midnight. When everyone had left the room, I was sitting by the window waiting for the henna paint to dry. The house was still buzzing with the sound of guests getting themselves comfortable and settled for the night.

My mother walked into the room with some food on a plate and she sat next to me and was very nice to me. Because she was really caring towards me, my eyes filled up with tears. I couldn't remember the last time she had been as affectionate as that. She was trying to hide her tears as well. She said to me, 'Well, only a few hours away and you'll be getting married and leaving us all to start a new life.' I felt very sad as I had never seen her that emotional before. I guess it was just the charged atmosphere in the house; it's probably quite natural around events such as weddings.

I had a little something to eat, then my mother left the room so I could get some rest. After she'd gone, something very strange happened. That night, there were still some last-minute guests arriving, and one of them was my mother's friend's son called Kabir. I hadn't seen him for ages, so I was surprised that he'd made the trip. He turned out to be very handsome as well. He sat on the edge of my bed, and we just couldn't stop talking, and he was cracking jokes every five minutes to make me laugh. He made me laugh so much that my stomach hurt! Then, out of the blue, he looked terribly serious and said to me, 'Don't marry somebody you don't love … marry me instead. I'll make you the happiest woman on this planet! You deserve a lot of happiness and more.'

At first, I thought that he was joking, as he had the habit of cracking jokes at the wrong time and place. But, as I looked at him, I realised that he was deadly serious. I didn't know what to say to him. He got down on his knees, held both of my hands and asked me again. He was so close to me that I could hear him breathing and, before I realised what I was doing, I put my hands through his hair and touched his face. For a few minutes, I completely forgot that I was already engaged and due to get married in a few hours!

Kabir got up and held me close to his chest, waiting for my answer. 'What are you thinking?' he asked.

I moved away from him and said sadly, 'It's impossible ... it would destroy my entire family. I can't hurt my father; he has been through enough organising this wedding.'

Kabir understood, but he was still set against my forthcoming marriage. He just kissed my forehead and left the room. Later, I discovered that he didn't want to stay for the wedding, so he had left. That was the last time I saw him.

I turned the lights off in the room. I was looking out through the window; it was very dark outside, softened with patches of moonlight. The light breeze caressed my face. I could see the decorations everyone had put up outside our house with all the beautiful lighting. I tried very hard not to think about what had just happened. I gazed out through the window and long into the distance, allowing my thoughts to wander, imagining what it would be like to be married to Kabir. I thought I would have been very happy. And then I must have fallen asleep.

4 THE LIVING DEAD

When the day of the wedding dawned, everyone started to get me ready for the main ceremony. It must have been at about 12.30pm that all the guests started to arrive at our house. The place was full of joy and happiness, and one by one all the guests came into my room to wish me well.

When the groom and his family arrived, everyone ran outside to see what the groom looked like, leaving me alone in the room. After a little while, when everyone had settled down, my friends came back to my room with all the clothes and gold jewellery that the groom had brought for me, according to our tradition. My friends helped me to put on the bright red wedding sari, embroidered with gold, and the outfit was finished with the matching gold jewellery.

There I was, looking every inch the bride. 'How do you feel?' my friends asked me. How could I possibly feel? I felt scared, just like an animal feels before it's slaughtered! That just about said it all.

Soon, the main marriage ceremony got under way. The groom and the Muslim cleric from the mosque were in a separate room. They then entered the room where I was sitting with two witnesses, as well as my close family and friends. That was when it really hit me – I realised that I was actually getting married.

A few tears rolled silently down my face, but no one saw them. The *imam* read a few things to me, to which I had to respond three times: 'Yes, I do.' Then he repeated the same thing for the groom ... and that was it: I was married.

Afterwards, my mother and brother brought me something to eat, but I couldn't eat anything, and then my father came into the room and, as soon as I saw him, I just burst into tears. He sat next to me and put his arms around me, and said, 'Please don't cry ... everything will be all right ...' but he couldn't even finish his sentence as he ended up in tears as well.

The final ceremony was to bring the bride and groom together, while everybody gave us their blessing. Nunu came and sat down next to me; he looked at me and smiled. I thought, 'Maybe he isn't as bad as I think he is.'

At about 4.30pm, it was time for me to leave my family home and go with Nunu and his family to his. This is perhaps the most emotional part of Asian weddings, one that all women find very hard to deal with. Up to this point, the woman's home has been constant, usually spent in the company of a close-knit family, and now, having got married, she has to leave all her family – and her former life – behind. Even though she can still visit her family whenever she wants, it's never the same from that moment on. So, whenever she visits her own family, she feels and is treated like a guest. All women find that extremely difficult to deal with at first, and then gradually they learn to accept the situation. I never did ... and I never will! My own family is my family – end of story. As long as I live, I'll never ever let any tradition, rules or any segregation come between my family and me.

One by one, everyone hugged me as they said goodbye to me, and when it was my parents' turn to say their farewells, they found it very hard. That was the first time I saw my mother crying for me. I was very touched by that, as you can imagine. My two older brothers were standing beside me trying to put on a brave face, but they couldn't hide their tears for too long, either.

I found it extremely hard to say goodbye to my little brother. I can still remember him saying to me, 'Do you have to go? Who is going to give me a bath when you are not here?' You can only imagine how sad I felt. Finally, my two brothers helped me into the car. I turned to look at them all as the car drove off.

Nunu's house wasn't too far from our own house, as they lived in the same town, so it only took half-an-hour to get there. In the car, Nunu didn't even try to comfort me, something I found quite strange, especially as I had just left my family.

When I arrived at his house, there were a huge number of people there who had all come to see the new bride. I felt very tired, a little dazed and under a lot of pressure, particularly because, from that moment, I had to accept this new family as my own. I had to adopt their way of life; I had to take on certain responsibilities as the daughter-in-law of their family. It was the start of my new life with a man I didn't even know or love! That thought sent a shiver up my spine.

By this time, I felt very hungry, but I couldn't ask for any food because, as a new bride, that's the last thing you want to do. You would rather die than say, 'I'm hungry,' which would be regarded as nothing but silly. Eventually, everyone left and Nunu's sister showed me to my room. I sat on a chair and thought of my family, wondering what they were doing. A little while later, Nunu's sister-in-law brought me something to eat, but I suddenly had no appetite for some reason.

I was alone in the room when Nunu came to see me, bringing me something sweet to eat. That was the first time he had ever sat down next to me and really talked to me. He said how beautiful I looked in my wedding dress, and asked if I was missing my family.

'Yes,' I said.

He took my hand and said, 'You'll be all right, because my family is your family now.'

I thought to myself, 'He seems a nice person, maybe I'll like him ...' but I didn't think that for long.

Out of the blue, he started to ask me very personal questions – had I had any boyfriends? Had I had any physical relationships with anyone before? And he asked me this despite knowing my family background.

'Look,' I said, 'this is an arranged marriage ... we don't even know each other, so I think we should get to know each other first.'

He wasn't very happy when he heard that. He said, 'Look, we are married now and we can talk about whatever we like ... you are my wife now.'

And, with that, the bastard started to put me under a lot of pressure. I didn't know how to react to that and, before I knew it, he started to become aggressive physically, and tried to make love to me. I'm not going to describe in detail everything that happened to me after that, simply because I feel disgusted and degraded even thinking about it, as many victims would. Only I will know how I was mentally and physically sickened that night by that animal. In the space of a few hours, my new husband had made me feel that my life wasn't worth living.

I didn't sleep at all that night. I think I was in a state of deep shock. At one point, I even thought of quietly slipping out of the room and running away as far as I could. But all hope was pointless – there was nowhere to go. So I got out of bed and sat in the corner of the room, on the floor, while he slept. I felt as though that room had become a living hell – I was frightened and shaking like a leaf, and wasn't sure when Nunu would wake up again. I sat there until the morning while the bastard lay there sleeping.

As I got up to go to the bathroom to wash my face, I found it difficult to move as I had a really high temperature. My stomach, my right breast and the side of my neck were extremely painful and inflamed, thanks to Nunu's treatment of me the night before.

He eventually woke up and came to sit next to me. He said, 'I'm sorry I was a bit nasty to you last night ... it won't happen again.'

I thought, 'What an animal! How can he treat me like that and then just say sorry?' I locked myself in the bathroom; I just couldn't stand there and take any more humiliation. I wasn't crying at all, I just wanted to be free of everything. I wished that it had simply been a nightmare, and that I would wake up in the morning like any other day and all would be normal again. Since that incident, every night I felt like a living corpse, and became alive again in the morning to face another day.

Women all over the world have so many dreams and happy memories of their wedding day. And me? Mine had become a nightmare already. I decided not to tell anyone about how he'd abused me because I felt deeply embarrassed; I'm sure most Asian women would have felt the same. And anyway, what would be the point? I was married to him now. I was born to suffer until I died. Who cared what happened to me anyway? No one did ... it took me a while to realise that, but it was true. The sooner I accepted that, the better it would be for me.

Somehow, I found enough strength to pull myself together. On the first full day of our married life, I still had to go through some more ceremonies throughout the day relating to our wedding – there was another party, more guests to meet, and I had to be very nice to Nunu's side of the family and their friends. All I had to do was smile and look very happy, which was very difficult after what had happened to me.

During one quiet moment, Nunu took me aside and whispered, 'Look, I said I'm sorry ... what more do you want? So please smile for the guests and the camera!' There he was, happy as anything, and flirting with some young girls, trying to make me jealous. But how could I possibly be jealous when I didn't even like him, never mind love him? In fact, he would have done me a favour if he'd gone after another woman; at least he wouldn't have had the time to come after me!

Somehow, I managed to get through the day. Don't misunderstand me – these were exceptional circumstances, and not what normally happens. In an ordinary, loving, happy marriage, I would have enjoyed the whole range of ceremonies and traditions, because our Asian weddings are full of fun when the couple are happy. But my wedding – and my husband – were far from 'normal'.

The next day, I was a little happier, because my parents were coming to invite Nunu and me back to their house to stay for few days, a practice that formed the last part of the official ceremony. So my family duly arrived and, after a meal, I left with them.

Unfortunately, Nunu accompanied me but, as soon as I walked into our house, I told him to give me some space because I needed to spend some time with my family. My mother took one look at me and asked me why I looked so ill. She knew straight away that something wasn't right. So she asked me again how I'd managed to make myself ill after only a couple of days.

My father sat next to me as well. I broke down in tears and told them that I didn't want to go back with Nunu because the man was an animal. Then I showed them some of the bruises on my body; they couldn't believe their eyes. My father was beside himself with rage. He told Nunu that he should go back to his house and give us some time to think things through.

Even though I had my family's support, it was a very unsettling and difficult time for me as I didn't know which direction my life was going to take. I even thought of running away and living the life of a renegade like my hero, Phoolan Devi. Obviously, this wasn't realistic but, if I'd really wanted it badly enough, I could have done something to turn my situation around. One thing was certain –

thinking about Devi gave me a lot of strength. I managed to stay at our family home for two weeks and refused to go back to Nunu's house, but deep down I knew that I would have to return eventually.

As time went on, I almost convinced myself that I would never have to go back to live with Nunu. I was beginning to enjoy staying in my own house with my family. And one of the most amazing aspects of this was that my mother and I became very close, and she started treating me quite differently. It was almost as dramatic as a miracle, and it made me very happy. I suspect, like many parents, my mother believed that young women become more mature after they get married. For the first time in my life, I was able to enjoy all the normal things mothers and daughters usually do together. We went shopping with all the money I received as part of my wedding gift; I cooked my mother's favourite dishes for her; I looked after her, and we even gossiped together like a couple of old fishwives!

While I was coping with the sadness my new life had brought, my family was also still struggling to survive financially. In fact, after all the money my father had spent on my wedding, the situation was very bad indeed. I realised that certain members of my family were trying to hide that from me, as they didn't want to upset me, but they couldn't keep it from me for too long. One day, I noticed that my mother was stitching an old pair of my little brother's trousers. I said to her that they were too threadbare, that she should just throw them away, and even if she managed to repair them they wouldn't last for long, but, before she could say anything, my little brother came into the room and said, 'Please don't throw them away! It's the only pair of trousers I've got!'

I looked at my mother as she told him off for letting the cat out of the bag. 'What on earth is going on?' I asked. 'Please tell me the truth …'

She hesitated; she didn't want me to be upset, she said, as I had my own problems. She didn't really have to tell me anything;

43

eventually, I saw it all with my own eyes. It wasn't only my little brother who had to wear ripped old clothes. My elderly father had to wear a pair of shoes which had a big hole in them, and my brother Raj was sleeping on an almost broken bed.

I thought about the fact that, in my house, each member of my family was struggling to survive, while Nunu's family was enjoying the brand-new furniture given to him by my father, as a sort of dowry. They didn't really need any furniture from us, as they were a very rich family. If they wanted to, they could simply have refused to accept the gift from my father. I felt like going back to Nunu's house with a large delivery van, loading up all the furniture given to them by my father, and bringing it all back to our house. But I couldn't really do that; my hands were tied. I was helpless.

As the financial difficulties began to bite, the relationships among various members of my family began to break down as well. I'm sure that it's not unusual for human relationships to suffer when there's a financial crisis in a home. There was certainly a great deal of tension and anger in the house at the time. My parents were arguing all the time, blaming each other for everything. Then brother Raj would argue with my father and, at times, these disagreements became more heated and violent. It was frightening to witness this, and I feared for what might happen in the future, because of Raj's aggressive behaviour.

I came to realise that, because the financial difficulties were causing so much pain, I couldn't expect them to take on my problems as well. I simply couldn't justify that. I think that's when the 'Goddess of Sacrifice' stirred within me. I just knew I had to do something to reduce my family's problems. I decided that I wasn't going to go against my family's decision if they sent me back to Nunu. At least that way they would have one less problem to worry about. That was one of the hardest decisions I've ever had to make in my life.

Two weeks later, Nunu's older brother came to see my father to sort things out and to take me back to their house. My father told him, 'It's not easy because my daughter has suffered a lot of abuse from Nunu. I won't be able to ask for a divorce for my daughter because she has only been married for a few weeks. No one will marry her after that ... you people almost destroyed her life.' Nunu's brother somehow managed to convince my father with his charm and flattery that everything would be all right, and so it was decided ... I had to go back.

After arriving back at Nunu's family home, I decided to carry on life as normally as possible. I said to myself that I was a Bangladeshi woman and I shouldn't forget that. 'I'll put everything into this marriage ... see if I can love him and make the marriage work.'

For a few days, Nunu didn't come anywhere near me, but his family started to give me a hard time over all sorts of trivial things. Why did I have too much pride? Why didn't I love Nunu just like any normal wife would? Who did I think I was, a queen or something? I then knew that they'd start making my life very difficult.

Despite everything, I carried on as normal, and the only major problem I faced was that I couldn't love Nunu even a tiny bit, no matter how hard I tried. I tried and tried, may God be my witness, I tried with all my strength. I carried on life in the hope that love might grow in my heart one day. But how could I possibly love someone who was willing to behave in such a disgusting way? It's not humanly possible. I was desperately, helplessly trapped in that marriage.

Occasionally, I was allowed to go and stay with my family, which I used to love. My mother used to cook all my favourite foods, and my older brother would take time off from work and come to meet me. I loved seeing my father as well, and I gained a lot of strength from spending time with him. I've learned so much from him. My close family always says I'm exactly like my father, as far as my personality is concerned. I consider that a wonderful compliment, as I'd say my father was the most intelligent, strong-minded, kindest man I've ever known.

I'll always remember one bit of advice from my father – 'If someone kicks you in your face, don't kick them back. Instead, ask that person, "Did you hurt your foot when you kicked me?"' At that time, I didn't really understand the meaning of this, but, believe me, I perfectly understand the meaning now! My father's views on life, and his advice to me, are priceless – you couldn't buy them with all the riches in the world.

5 LEAVING HOME

Seven months went by while Nunu's family was preparing our visas and passports for our journey to England. As the time drew nearer, I started to feel frightened because I didn't know how I'd survive without my family. I would be thousands of miles away from my family and friends, living with one of Nunu's older brothers and his family. The thought sent shivers up and down my spine. I didn't even have any family or friends in England.

But, at the same time, somewhere in my heart I felt that there might be a chance of happiness for me in England. Maybe Nunu would change and start loving me, or maybe I'd start loving him. Lots of possibilities went through my mind, in what was undoubtedly an attempt to reassure myself that everything would be all right.

During the run-up to our life abroad, something strange happened. As usual one morning, I made breakfast for Nunu and went to wake him up. He told me to go away and leave him alone because he wanted to get some more sleep. So I just shut the door behind me and left him alone, thinking little of it. This happened for a few days, during which time he became progressively more moody and angry. I tried to talk to him, but that didn't work either.

On the fourth day, he woke up just before midday and, after breakfast, I asked him whether I could go to my father's house, because I would like to spend some more time with my family before going to England, as I would probably not get to see them for a very long time. He said to me, 'You are married now and this is your house, not your father's house! Stay here until nearer the time … then you can go and see your family.'

Then his mother jumped into the conversation and started to shout at me, saying things like, 'You're not fit to be a good wife. Didn't your family teach you anything?'

I just couldn't take any more of that type of behaviour, so I became really upset and said to Nunu that I wasn't going to eat anything until he took me to my father's house. I told him that I had every right to spend some time with them before I went to England. I didn't realise that, by saying that, my worst nightmare would become reality. Nunu became very angry, dragged me from my chair and started to push me. As if that wasn't enough, he shouted things like, 'You're a waste of space! You don't do as you're told!' Then he pushed me out of the room and told me to get out of the house.

I collapsed outside on the doorstep, sobbing. After a few minutes, Nunu came out in a towering rage, jabbed a finger at my face and growled, 'Stop crying or I will divorce you now! Then you can go back to your family for good! You will never have to come back!'

I still remember after he said that that I felt as though the whole world was crumbling around me, as though there had been a sort of earthquake. I was left completely numb.

The reason for this was one of the words Nunu had used – 'divorce'. In our culture, when two people are married, if there is a major problem and they don't get on well, either of them has the right to get divorced. For a man, he need only say 'I divorce you' three times in front of two witnesses and, if he means it from his heart, the marriage is no longer valid. For a woman to divorce a man, however, the process is quite different.

In my case, if Nunu wanted a divorce because I didn't love him, he had the right to go through with it. But divorce is by no means an easy option for couples – it signifies failure and shame – so it is especially hurtful and insulting for a husband to threaten his wife with 'divorce' every time he loses his temper with her. In fact, some people believe that there is no worse insult. In some parts of Bangladesh, I've heard countless stories of women committing suicide after their husbands had threatened to divorce them over and over again.

After Nunu's threat, he just went completely mad. He glared at me, turned and then slammed the door behind him, before sloping off to his mother's room. I could hear him telling her that I wasn't good enough to be anybody's wife, or even pretty enough! I was surprised that his mother didn't try to stop him saying that. Then I could hear him coming back to where I was, saying, 'I'll throw her out of this house … Why doesn't she just die?' By then, his older brother managed to stop him from reaching me.

I just covered my ears with my hands; after hearing all that, I just wished I could end my life there and then. I just didn't want to hear any more. His mother came into the room and told me not to leave because she needed to check with the *imam* whether our marriage was still valid or not. As Nunu had clearly used the word 'divorce', and others may have heard him, there was some doubt in her mind about whether we were still officially married.

When I realised that she was serious, I couldn't stop crying, as I felt I'd been abused and dehumanised in so many ways. All I could see was a future filled with darkness, and my whole body went cold.

My mother-in-law left the room to call the *imam* and, shortly after he arrived, she ordered me to get up, but I didn't have enough strength left in my body. She dragged me by my arm and then dropped me at the *imam*'s feet. Then she said, 'You should ask for the cleric's forgiveness first. Sit there 'til you are asked to move!'

I just sat there like a disobedient child waiting to be punished. I felt that they had all managed to strip away my last bit of dignity. I felt so sick but I was too scared even to throw up.

At first, the *imam* informed me that what had happened had been entirely my fault. I kept quiet, because physically and mentally I didn't have the strength to talk back. As things turned out, it appeared that I had been 'lucky'. Because there had been no official witnesses present when Nunu had mentioned divorce, the marriage was still valid. Things calmed down a bit soon after that, but I never dared mention going to my father's house again.

Can you imagine how insulted I felt? After that incident, nothing mattered to me any more. There were no weapons left for him to hurt me with. No matter what he might do to me from then on, no insult or attack would ever be as bad as the one I had just experienced.

A week later, I got the visa to go to England. As soon as I heard about my visa, I became even more frightened. I reckoned that, if Nunu could do that to me while I was in Bangladesh, what would he be capable of in England? I didn't have anyone to go to in England, so what would I do? I came up with a plan: when they let me go and visit my family, I'd tell my father that I wanted to get out of the marriage. I'd tell him that it was simply unbearable for me. Then I'd get a job or something to support myself, so that way I wouldn't be a burden to them.

Eventually, I was allowed to go and visit my family a week before I was due to leave for England. I immediately told them the whole story about Nunu and his family's treatment of me, and they were very upset and angry, but they didn't know what to do or how to help the situation. All they could do, they felt, was try to talk to Nunu and his family to see what should be done for the best.

Up until then, I hadn't told them about my decision to ask for a divorce from Nunu. I felt it was important to wait for the right moment, as divorce was the very last path to take in an unsuccessful marriage. I had been brought up to believe that, and I still felt that that was the case.

Later on that evening, my seven-year-old brother came and sat next to me. 'Sister,' he said, 'could you send me a lot of clothes and toys when you go to England? All my friends have nice clothes and I only have two pairs! And, by the time you go to England, the ones I've got will be old and torn. I also want you to send me a school bag, because I only have a plastic bag at the moment to carry my books to school.'

I swear, when I heard him saying this, it made me realise how selfish I had been. Believe me, my problems seemed trivial compared to those of my little brother. I instantly regretted ever thinking that I should tell my family that I wanted a divorce. What sort of person was I? I would only have added another problem to the long list they already had. I prayed silently, 'Please, God, forgive me for being such a selfish person, and give me the opportunity to be strong.' From then on, I found some inner strength from somewhere, and I felt I could face anything that Nunu put me through.

I decided to forget about the possibility of a divorce. First things first, I needed to raise some money somehow before I left. After a lot of thinking, I went to two of my best friends, and borrowed a large amount of money. I told them that, once I was in England, and assuming I stayed alive, one day they would get their money back. And I did manage to repay all the money eventually ... it only took me eight years!

I gave the money to my mother, and told her not to tell my father or he wouldn't accept it. His pride was everything to him. At least that would help until things started to get better. My mother told me off for borrowing such an enormous amount of money, but she accepted it anyway.

With only four days to go until I left for England, everyone was very upset. They couldn't believe that I was leaving them and going so far away. I decided to forget about Nunu and enjoy the next four days with my family. Let's face it, only God knew when I'd see them again. Of all the people I'd miss, I knew the one who meant the most to me – my father.

During those four days, I felt even closer to every single member of my family. We went shopping together, talked openly about things and visited different places together. They weren't the same family they used to be. I thought to myself how cruel destiny could be – for the first time in my life, I'd found a new level of love and respect within my own family, and now I had only a few days before leaving them, possibly for ever. I might not even see my parents again.

I realised that my father was not going to be the same man again after I left. I helped my little brother as much as I could with little things that he needed. I simply took money from Nunu, saying that I needed this and that for the journey. I have no guilt over that because, by giving Nunu the dowry, my father suffered enormously.

With only three days left before the flight, I found that I just couldn't eat or sleep. It's impossible to describe the emotional turmoil as I prepared to leave the country where I was born and brought up. The enormity of my situation really hit home as I contemplated saying goodbye to my family and friends, and particularly my elderly father. I tried to cope with the upset, but I felt heartbroken. Outwardly, though, I tried to remain positive. I visited all of my close relatives and friends before I left, and the goodbyes became harder and harder.

Finally, the day arrived. I got up very early and stood outside on the balcony of our house. For a few minutes, I had the horrific feeling that I might never return to stand in the same spot again. I went into the garden, picked up some sand and put that in a plastic bag to take with me to England. Who knew when I'd see Bangladesh again? My father came and stood next to me and put his arms around me to offer some comfort.

At midday, Nunu arrived to pick me up. My family accompanied us to the coach station because they were coming to the airport the next day. All except my father – he didn't want to come to the airport because he couldn't bear to see me walking away from him with his own eyes, so he preferred to say his farewells when we boarded the coach.

Once there, I just couldn't hide my tears any more, and broke down crying. My entire family were in tears as well. I kept on saying to my father as I was crying, 'I don't want to go because I won't see any of you any more … please, don't let me go … I don't have anyone in England, I want to stay here.'

My father kept saying, 'Don't worry, my prayers are with you … nothing will happen to you.' I remember the very last thing my father said to me: 'I know you will find your happiness in England. So don't forget that, all you need to do is to believe in yourself … don't ever let go of your hope.'

Then Nunu guided me on to the coach and sat me down. Then, slowly, the coach edged away from the bus station; I could still see my father through the window, standing there. I wondered if that was the last time I'd ever see him.

Even now, 14 years later, whenever I close my eyes, I can still see him standing there for me. Sometimes, I can even imagine him coming back to that same spot to welcome me if I ever return to Bangladesh.

I have to admit, Nunu showed some compassion towards me on the journey for a change. When we finally arrived in Dhaka, we stayed in a hotel near the airport. I asked Nunu and his older brother if I could go to my uncle's house where my mother and brothers were staying, as it was only three miles from the hotel. But Nunu angrily snapped 'No', and his older brother started to shout at me, 'Hey, you are not the only woman who's leaving her family and going abroad! So enough is enough! You can't go there!'

So that was it; I had to stay in the hotel. I wasn't sure, but I thought that the real reason they didn't let me go was because they thought I might not come back. I couldn't sleep that night at all; I was filled with thoughts of my family and was unable to stop crying.

In the morning, I threw up a few times in the toilet, which must have been something to do with the anxiety. I then got ready in a daze, and left the hotel with Nunu and his brother. Ten minutes later, we arrived at Zia International Airport, named after one of the late Bangladeshi presidents. I got out of the car and, as soon as I saw my family waiting there, I just ran to them. Nunu came after me and said we'd only got half-an-hour, then we had to check in. Then I spent my last half-hour with my family. Eventually, I had to join Nunu in the terminal, and that was when I was forced to say goodbye, and leave them. I kept on looking back as I walked away, just to catch glimpses of them for as long as I could. I shouted to them on the other side of the glass, 'I'll come back soon!' My mother looked at me as though she wasn't ever going to see me again. I waved to them until I couldn't see them any more, as they had disappeared into the crowd in the terminal building.

My little brother's last words echoed in my mind. Just before I left, he asked me which toy car I would bring him when I returned to Bangladesh. Now my little brother is in his twenties! I haven't seen my family for 14 years! I still have that little toy car I bought for him, as I want to give it to him personally.

We boarded the plane. Nunu sat next to me and put his arms around me to comfort me, but, strangely, I wasn't crying. I just felt empty. It was as if I'd decided that, if I had leave my family, I was ready to face anything ... so, come on then, what's next?

The plane took off; I didn't know what to feel any more. I had only a vague hope that I'd find some happiness in England, and then I fell asleep. We had to stop in Bahrain in the Middle East for the night to change flights, so we went to a hotel. The next day, we boarded another plane and then flew straight to England. I arrived in England, at Heathrow Airport, on 5 June 1990.

As soon as I got off the plane, I felt very ill and had to go to the toilet to throw up. It must have been because of the long journey, I thought. Nunu started to tell me off as usual, saying, 'What's wrong with you? Why are you being sick? It's bloody embarrassing in front of people! Are you pregnant or something?' I didn't think for a second that I was pregnant, because I had no idea at all what being pregnant might feel like.

One of the officials at the airport was standing nearby and he saw that I was having difficulty walking. So he asked me if everything was all right, but I didn't know what to say to him because, at that time, I couldn't speak any English at all. Even if I had understood him, I would have remained silent because Nunu was with me. Nunu explained to the member of staff that I was feeling sick and that he didn't know what to do with me.

The official then took us to a room where I could rest for a while, and I thought it was nice of him to do that. After a little bit of a rest, I felt a lot better. Then I had to prepare myself to meet one of Nunu's older brothers and his wife, who would be putting us up while we settled in England. That was nerve-wracking, as I'd never spoken to them or met them, and Nunu made things worse by telling me to cover my head properly as they were his older brother and sister-in-law. They were waiting to meet us outside the airport, so we left the Customs area quickly and met up with them. Both seemed nice people, as they immediately made me feel comfortable. I thought that was a good start.

They lived in Birmingham, in the centre of England, so a few hours later we arrived at their house, and met their two children. I must admit, I felt fine for some strange reason, and started to believe that things could get better between Nunu and me with his family around because he wouldn't treat me badly. He might even treat me like human being for a change.

Two days went by, and I was dying to talk to my family on the phone but felt a bit awkward asking my hosts if I could use their phone. Eventually, Nunu's brother said that he thought I should phone my family in Bangladesh to let them know we'd arrived safely. I felt really happy and phoned them.

It was wonderful to hear their voices. First, I spoke to my father, then the others. They were delighted to hear from me, and all the while I tried not to cry, as I didn't want my family to think that I was unhappy. After that phone call, I didn't speak to my family for ages, because the offer to make a call wasn't made, and I wasn't going to ask, because it's not in my nature to ask for things. But I wrote to them regularly, instead, and they wrote back as well.

A few weeks later, I became ill. I couldn't eat at all, and constantly felt sick. It didn't take a genius to work out that I was pregnant. I felt very happy, as it was my own baby I was carrying, and was part of my own body. At the same time, I felt sad knowing the sort of father the baby was going to have.

I was frightened to death, as this was my first pregnancy; I didn't know what to expect. Nunu's sister-in-law was pregnant as well at that time, so I guess that made me feel a little bit better, in that I wasn't alone.

I wrote to my family, giving them the news about my pregnancy, and they were very happy for me. The first few weeks were very easy for me, as I wasn't under any pressure from Nunu or his family. All I had to do was to be very polite to my in-laws, and, whenever guests came to see me as Nunu's new bride, I just had to make lots of cups of tea. That was not a terribly difficult job!

Within a few weeks, Nunu started to work with his brother in a Bangladeshi restaurant as a chef. He used to go to work at 4.30pm and would return at 2.00am. My routine was to get up in the morning, prepare the breakfast, and then at about 11.30am they would all get up, then sometimes I had to take Nunu's breakfast up to the bedroom. The worst part of the day was midday, because I had to help Nunu's sister-in-law with the cooking. That was difficult, simply because everything we made or used was very different from what I was used to in Bangladesh, ranging from the meals themselves to the herbs and spices we added – it took me a good few months to get used it all. But, slowly, I learned everything.

Getting used to such a different way of life and environment all in one go was not easy, especially as I still couldn't read or write English. One day, Nunu's sister-in-law sent me to their corner shop to buy some chocolates. When I got back, I gave her the shopping bag and, after she'd taken out the shopping, she looked at me in disbelief. Slowly, it became clear what I'd actually bought.

'Dog biscuits!' she screamed, completely losing it. 'You stupid fool … don't you know the difference between chocolates and bloody dog biscuits?'

She was right – I *didn't* know the difference! I felt really embarrassed. As soon as I'd gone into the shop, I'd looked at them and thought to myself that they looked really delicious, and automatically I assumed that they were chocolates. Not being able to speak or read English didn't help, either, and I had never seen dog biscuits while I was in Bangladesh. Now I wish I had fed those dog biscuits to Nunu … by mistake, obviously!

At times, I found myself feeling very lonely. I used to sit by the bedroom window and look out for hours; I felt trapped. I wanted to get out into the big, wide world and discover for myself what was out there. How wonderful it would be to know that there was somebody out there, who would love me and comfort me, somebody to hold me in his arms and hide me from all the pain. I wondered if anybody was out there for me, or would I have to spend the rest of my life with Nunu? How could I ever force myself to love him when he chose to treat me with such contempt?

Sometimes, I would look at the couples in the street and wish I had someone to hold my hand and walk with. And I counted my • lucky stars that Nunu's brother was such a kind and caring man. He was very good-looking, and I respected him a great deal as a person. He was exactly the opposite of Nunu, but I never had any feelings for him other than regarding him like a older brother. In our culture, I had accepted the traditional custom of treating my husband's brothers like my own.

As the days went by, I had to go to the hospital for my regular ante-natal check-ups. One day, I went to the hospital for my first ultrasound scan. I didn't know what to expect. I was feeling a little frightened and bewildered, so I asked Nunu to come with me. He replied that he didn't feel comfortable going to that sort of thing, as it was a female matter. So he told his brother and the sister-in-law to take me.

When I got to the hospital, I had a great deal of trouble with the doctors, as I couldn't speak English. They couldn't understand me, and I couldn't understand them. I felt so helpless and embarrassed, I started to panic.

The doctor must have felt sorry for me, so he held my hand and tried to comfort me, then he called Nunu's brother into the room to translate for me. It was so embarrassing for me to have Nunu's older brother explaining personal things to the doctor on my behalf, but I had no choice as his wife couldn't speak English, either. Whatever my feelings on the matter, it was something that simply had to be done.

That day after I came home, I asked Nunu if he would help me somehow to learn English. As soon as I said that, he burst out laughing. 'You want to learn English?' he asked in a very patronising way. 'You haven't even got a brain to be a good wife and you want to learn English? Forget about learning English … just learn the cooking and that will do.' That day, just as he had done on many occasions, he made me feel insignificant and worthless through his petty insults and patronising attitude.

The only time he was nice to me was when he wanted to get close to me physically, and even then he used to make fun of a particular part of my body. He even compared me to English women, and commented that I didn't have white skin like them! Once he said to me that, if I'd been like a certain actress, he would have loved me from head to toe. I just used to lower my face and listen to his bullshit, what else could I do? The last time I stood up to him was when I was in Bangladesh, and I remembered all too vividly what had happened. He had threatened to divorce me, and I didn't want to go through another divorce drama.

Six months passed; I was missing my family. I was in touch with them through letters, but I was dying to speak to them on the phone. That wasn't always possible, as it was very expensive. I had a letter one day from my father saying that, since I had left Bangladesh, everything had started to fall apart. He said I was their lucky star. I knew that they were missing me as well, and thought that there's probably a lot of truth in the saying 'You don't know what you've got 'til it's gone.'

I wanted to do something to help my family, so I hatched a little plan when I heard that Nunu's friend's father was going to Bangladesh, and he was due to come and see Nunu before he left. When no one was looking, I gave him £100 to give to my brother Raj. I'd managed to save it up whenever Nunu's brother or his wife gave me some spending money. The man was very nice, and didn't tell anyone in the house about that. I would have been in big trouble otherwise! This was because, according to Nunu, your husband's family was everything, and your family in Bangladesh should mean nothing to you. What a selfish little bastard he was ... and probably still is! I used to help my own family whenever I could, and I decided that, if anyone was going to object to that, that would be the beginning of World War III as far as I was concerned.

6 SECRETS AND LIES

I never knew that a smile from a stranger would give me so much strength. Some days, after Nunu went to work, I used to go up to my bedroom and stand by the window and gaze out into the world beyond the curtains. That was the only time I could be on my own and relax for a while.

As usual, I was looking across the road and noticed that an Asian man was looking at me through the window of the house opposite. As I looked at him, he smiled at me. I felt very shy and hid behind the curtain. Perhaps it was the fact that I was still new to England, but I just didn't feel comfortable making contact with people I didn't know. A few seconds later, I peered out from behind the curtain, but he wasn't there.

The next day, the same thing happened again. We couldn't talk because, even though his house was opposite ours, it was still too far to shout across the road. And anyway, being a married woman, I wouldn't have dared talk to another man that way, even though I wasn't happily married. My upbringing wouldn't allow me to do that.

Eventually, both of us plucked up enough courage to attempt a sort of sign language. He asked me how I was. I replied the same way, saying, 'I'm all right.' Within a few days of this exchange, we become good friends. It was funny, really, because, whenever Nunu's sister-in-law entered the room, we used to pretend that we didn't know each other! Then, as soon as she'd gone, we'd both start laughing. We never spoke, but our eyes did all the talking.

One day, I had to go shopping with Nunu's sister-in-law, so we had to walk down the road and past his house. And would you believe it, I saw him standing at his gate. We looked at each other, but he didn't have a clue who I was as I was wearing my veil. I had to cover up my head whenever I went out, because that was what Nunu and his family wanted; I had no choice in that.

Of course, I wouldn't dream of criticising any Muslim women who choose to wear the *hijab*. I'm a Muslim woman myself, but I choose not to wear the *hijab* now or practise Islam as much as other more observant Muslims do. I do value Islam as well as all religions in the world, but I don't have to justify my choices to anybody, only to God. Just because I don't pray five times a day or wear the *hijab* doesn't mean that I'm not a good Muslim. I do pray in my mind all the time to God. And, whenever I see a picture of a pilgrim or a holy Muslim site or even when I go to an Islamic bookshop, I certainly feel a kind of peace in my heart. It's like being very close to something wonderful, but not quite being able to reach it. Whenever I see a Hindu temple or a Christian church, I feel exactly the same. When you think about it, all religion has one thing in common – the fact that we all must use our common sense. If we all used this, it makes perfect sense not to lie, not to hurt others, to respect your elders, not to kill and so on. But, in everyday life, these most basic principles are so easily forgotten.

To be honest with you, I believe that we should practise the religion of 'humanity' first, and then the world would become a slightly better place. It might be only then that we would be able to accept each other more readily. I always say, 'Accept me for what I am without any discrimination, and you'll have a friend for life.'

Islam itself is a very peaceful religion; and, yes, there are people out there who use Islam as an excuse, or even take Islam to an extreme. I personally don't have any time for them; they give Islam a very bad name. True Muslim people, people who know and study Islam, truly know how beautiful Islam can be. They have a direct connection with God. People who don't know anything about Islam shouldn't criticise the religion without first studying it. By the same token, I wouldn't criticise other religions, because I equally respect all the other world faiths, as they all have the same principles at heart.

Above all else, the most powerful religion on this planet is 'love'. I believe that, with love, we can achieve anything, even God.

As far as that 'relationship' with the man in the window was concerned, I never really knew what sort of connection we had had – maybe some relationships don't have to have names. Even though I liked him, I used to feel guilty admitting that to myself. After all, I was a married woman. No matter what, I wouldn't forget my values. It's our values that give us our individuality and, without our values, we don't have any self-respect.

I was seven months pregnant at the time, and one day I went out with Nunu to get some groceries from the shop. When we got there, I just couldn't believe my eyes … the man from over the road was in the shop as well. Sometimes, when I went out with Nunu, I didn't bother wearing my *hijab*, and this day was one of those days. As he looked at me, he saw that I was in the shop with Nunu, and he also noticed that I was unmistakably pregnant! He also probably guessed that I was married to Nunu. I looked into his eyes; I could see he wanted to say so much to me, and how much he wanted to love me.

After that chance meeting, the following day Nunu sent me to the shop to get a pack of cigarettes for him. And I saw him again! He just came up to me and smiled and, as he came close to me, he said, 'Hello.' I felt as though my heart had skipped a beat. He stood very close to me and said, 'I never thought I'd come this close to you.' Then, very gently, he touched my belly and said, 'Look after yourself.'

I think I just froze. That was the gentlest way anyone has ever touched me. It was almost like touching a flower. It was reassuring to know that there are still some nice men left in this world ... but only some.

If I think of that encounter today, it seems that the man was God-sent into my empty life to give me a glimpse of light. He had the most amazing eyes; I could see love in his eyes for me from afar. I'm sure all women harbour dreams of being specially loved and cared for by their husbands during pregnancy. Well, I had none of that.

The sad thing was that, sometimes, I used to crave a little bit of affection from a loving man, somebody to hold me tight, close to his heart; somebody whom I could just cuddle up to and go to sleep with ... and awake in the morning listening to his heartbeat; somebody who would make me feel like a complete woman emotionally. Was that too much to ask for? I don't think so ... I never gave up hope and never will.

Some nights, I used to sit by myself and try to put some oil on my legs and my big belly, because during my pregnancy the skin on my belly used to feel itchy, which, I suppose, is something most pregnant women experience.

Nunu never bothered to look after me, not that I particularly wanted him to. But it would at least have been a decent thing for him to do, to care for his pregnant wife when she needed it. On the contrary, Nunu seemed to delight in humiliating me, and decided one day, on his day off, to tell me to get ready, because he wanted to take me to the cinema. I thought to myself that at least it would be a chance to get out of the house.

So we went to the centre of Birmingham, got the tickets for the cinema, walked in and sat down. The movie started, and it was in English. It soon became obvious that this was a very particular kind of English movie – sort of pornographic! I could not believe how insensitive he was! How could he bring me to the cinema to watch something like that? I felt so embarrassed my face went bright red. I said to him, 'What do you think you are doing? Let's go and watch another movie.'

'We are not going anywhere,' he replied. 'Why, are you shy? You are my wife. Look at the other English couples; they are not shy, they are doing what they like.'

I said, 'I know I'm your wife, but is there any reason for humiliating me like this in public? And I'm not an Englishwoman, am I?'

I couldn't get through to him at all. I just had to sit there quietly all the way through the film, and suffer the indignity and humiliation in silence. I didn't say anything else to him, as I didn't want to make things worse for myself. So I tried my best to sit with him, trying to be as normal as I could, and tried to block out the excruciating back pain that had been brought on by the pregnancy.

When we finally got home, I locked myself in the bathroom and burst into tears of shame. That night, as I had done on other occasions, I wished I was dead.

My problem is that I completely, 100 per cent believe in love. I do not believe that you need to sit in a cinema and watch a pornographic movie to have a healthy relationship. And I was not in love with Nunu at all. So it was extremely difficult for me to accept and endure his sick appetites. You wouldn't humiliate someone you truly love like that. So I guess I should probably have expected him to do something like that, because he never had any respect for me whatsoever.

As far as I was concerned, two people's sex life is something extremely private, and should not be made public. Whatever they do behind closed doors, it's their business. It's their choice if they want to make it public, fair enough. But for Nunu to humiliate me like that in public was shocking and deeply upsetting for me. I tried to tell Nunu's sister-in-law but she didn't show any interest in helping me. I could have talked to his older brother, but I felt embarrassed to talk about that subject. I liked him; he was kind and considerate towards me, and I'm sure he would have had a word with Nunu if I'd asked him.

Why is it that some people can always find the bad in things, instead of the good? One day, everyone in the house went to visit some relatives, except Nunu's older brother who remained at home with me. It was his day off, so he wanted to have a rest. I was in the kitchen because I had a lot of cooking to do, and Nunu's brother was sitting in the living room reading a newspaper. As I was cooking, I asked him if he wanted a cup of tea because I was making one. He came into the kitchen and said, 'Let me help you with your cooking.'

I was very surprised by that. In fact, I was shocked, and it reinforced the vast difference between Nunu and his brother. So he helped me with few things, and at one stage I was trying to move a very hot pan from the cooker when he stopped me and offered to do it himself.

Sadly, later on, when his wife found out that he'd been helping me in the kitchen, she became suspicious and tried to turn him against me. But there was no reason whatsoever for her to do that, because I never regarded him as anything other than an older brother. People say a lie never goes too far, but the truth is that some people do get away with lies. Such is life. I don't know why God was testing me so severely … I suppose I must have done something to upset Him!

After that incident, Nunu's sister-in-law changed her attitude towards me, and started to tell me off for the most trivial things. I asked Nunu a few times to have a word with her, but, instead of helping me, he told me to get used to it because she was his older sister-in-law, so it would be disrespectful for him to argue with her.

I knew deep down that he wouldn't help me, so I just carried on as normal.

One day, as usual, Nunu went to work, leaving me sitting in the living room reading a paper, trying to learn to speak English. Then, at about 7.30pm, Nunu walked in. I was surprised because he didn't usually return from work that early, so I asked him if he was all right. He said no, he wasn't feeling very well, and he wanted to be left alone. So I left him to his own devices.

The next day, after lunch, just as he was getting ready to go out, he sat on the sofa to put his shoes on. I think the shoelaces were knotted, and he was getting annoyed with them. He asked for my help, so I sat down on the floor to sort out the knot. Before I even realised that he'd completely lost his temper, he slapped me across my face, making me fall sideways. He shouted, 'What a useless idiot ... you can't even tie a shoelace properly!'

I can't begin to describe the level of anger welling up inside me. There and then I waned to slap him back as hard as I could. But how could I? I was a seven-and-a-half-month-pregnant woman!

The next day, I talked to his sister-in-law and told her that what happened. She told me he did get a little bit moody like that sometimes, and that I should just leave him alone for a while and he'd be all right. I did as I was told; I left him alone.

The following day, he woke up late and looked like a completely different person – very angry, detached, and didn't want to talk to anyone. I tried to talk to him but he told me to leave him alone, and he meant it. It was really strange behaviour, even for someone who was strange at the best of times, and his brother and sister-in-law seemed to accept it as a passing phase – I just didn't know what was happening or what to do for the best.

The following morning, Nunu's brother took him somewhere and came back with some medicine. I asked his brother what the medicine was for. He replied that Nunu had been working very hard for the last few months, and that was why he wasn't very well, so the doctor gave him the medication. Then Nunu's sister-in-law locked the medicine in a drawer in her bedroom.

A whole week passed with no discernible change in Nunu, so I started to become more and more suspicious, because I simply didn't know what was going on. Particularly strange was the fact that, whenever Nunu needed his medicine, his sister-in-law took it out of the drawer and gave it to him in her room. I began to wonder what it was they were hiding from me. Then again, I thought that maybe I was being unnecessarily paranoid – why on earth would they bother to hide something from me?

The following day, I had a nice letter from my father so I felt really happy. My father used to write to me twice a week, and the rest of my family wrote every two weeks, but my father never let me down. He was my biggest strength throughout that difficult time.

With two weeks gone, there was still no change in Nunu's behaviour; he was sleeping all day and most of the night and, when he was awake, he was in a foul mood with everyone in the house, especially me. It occurred to me that perhaps I was responsible for him being like that; after all, I knew very well that I never loved him. Loving Nunu would have been impossible!

I decided to talk to him, regardless of what might happen to me. I made a cup of tea and went up to the bedroom. Nunu was lying on the bed reading something and listening to music. I sat next to him on the bed, and asked him how he was feeling. I didn't get much from him, so I got quickly to the point. 'Have I done something or said something to upset you? Is that the reason you are like this?'

He didn't answer me directly; he simply repeated that he was ill and he wanted to be left alone.

He took a sip of tea and, within a split-second, I saw the other side of Nunu. He lost his temper and hurled the cup at me, shouting something about not putting enough sugar in it. I was so frightened that my whole body started to shake.

I got up and said I'd go downstairs and make him another cup. But he was still very angry and wouldn't stop shouting or swearing at me. I thought I'd better leave him, but I only managed to get halfway down the stairs before Nunu came after me. He slapped me and I lost my balance, falling to the bottom of the stairwell. As if that wasn't enough, he swore at me using the most hurtful language he could think of. Then Nunu's sister-in-law came running out to see what was going on, while I managed to pull myself into a sitting position on the stairs. I can still remember not wanting to move; I thought that, if I moved, I'd lose the baby. Then Nunu's sister-in-law started to tell him off for making so much noise!

Nunu turned on his sister-in-law, telling her to shut up, then he ordered me to get up and go to the bedroom and stay there. I got up somehow, climbed the stairs and went to sit on the floor of the bedroom in a corner. I was really frightened; I must have sprained my wrist because I was in terrible pain, and my back had started to hurt a little as well. Not having been in this situation before, I wasn't sure whether I was losing the baby. My entire body was shaking, and I felt very cold. I could hear Nunu downstairs arguing with his sister-in-law. Quickly, I got on the bed and covered myself with the blanket, as I tried to calm the rising panic and the shaking in my limbs.

Then I heard a few loud knocks on the door. I nearly had a heart-attack! I remained where I was, because I was too frightened to go to the door and God only knew what Nunu would do to me if I opened it. I started to cry, and then Nunu came into the bedroom, saying, 'Look what you've done! The police are here now. Because of you, next-door must have called the police!' Then, before I knew what was happening, he threw our small radio against the window, smashing half of the pane. Then he grabbed our wedding video, took a lighter out of his pocket, and started to set fire to it.

I seriously thought he was going to burn me next! I was crying and begging him not to hurt me. Then I heard somebody coming up the stairs, and two policemen appeared at the doorway. One of them grabbed Nunu and took him downstairs.

Somehow, I got up and sat down on the bed, but my body still wouldn't stop shaking. So the other officer put the blanket over me properly and put one of his arms around me. I think I felt safe; at least I knew that Nunu wouldn't come anywhere near me while the police were there. Then he tried to find out what had happened, so he asked me some questions, very politely, but I couldn't understand very much of what he said. I couldn't talk to the officer, so I just broke down in tears of frustration.

The officer realised that I didn't speak any English, so he just comforted me, and after a while Nunu's sister-in-law came into the room and said something to the police officer in her broken English. I didn't understand what she said, but after that the officer looked at me once more, then smiled and left the room. By then, they had arrested Nunu and taken him away.

Soon after that, all hell broke loose. Nunu's sister-in-law rang her husband at work to tell him what had happened, whereupon he came home and got very angry with me. I had never seen him that angry before, and I was really confused and scared when he shouted at me, 'Why did you have to make him angry when he's ill? We got him married to you so you could cure him, love him, not to make his condition worse. I hope you're satisfied with yourself!'

I was completely lost for words! I didn't have any idea what he was talking about. I wanted to ask him what on earth he meant, but seeing him that angry made me think that I shouldn't ask him anything. I was becoming more and more confused, wishing that somebody would tell me what was going on. I was feeling so cold and hungry by this time, but, while Nunu's brother was shouting, I didn't want to go downstairs to the kitchen. I sat on my bed in the dark, worrying about what was going to happen next, and why they were blaming me. What had I done? What had happened to Nunu? Why had they arrested him? I guessed it must have been because he'd been violent. What were they going to do with me? I also wondered if the baby was all right, because I usually felt the baby move a few times a day but, since all this had started, I hadn't felt the baby move at all.

At about midnight, I thought I'd go downstairs and talk to them, and find out once and for all what was happening. I also needed to have something to eat. I was so hungry that my stomach was burning with pain, so I carefully made my way downstairs, and saw Nunu's brother and his wife sitting in the living room. They were discussing something very quietly but, as soon as I entered the room, they stopped talking.

I didn't say a word immediately; I went into the kitchen and warmed up some food for them as well as myself. Nunu's sister-in-law then joined me in the kitchen, and finally asked me if I was feeling all right. I told her I only had a pain in my wrist and back, which could turn out to be nothing, but that I would like to see a doctor. She thought about that for a moment and said, 'Let's have something to eat, then I'll ask my husband to take you to the hospital.'

I asked her why the police had arrested Nunu, and where they had taken him. I made it clear that I simply wanted to know what was going on. All she said was that Nunu would be fine, and that we'd go and see him in the morning.

As we all sat round the dinner table to eat, Nunu's brother started to tell me off again, saying I was old enough to understand him better. 'You should have had more sense ... Haven't your parents taught you anything?' he said. Believe me, this was hurtful enough to make me feel I didn't want to eat another thing, but I still had that hunger pain, and felt that I should try to eat more for my own sake and that of my baby.

Eventually, they took me to the hospital and Nunu's sister-in-law said to me that they'd say to the doctor that I had had an accident, otherwise Nunu would be in even more trouble. 'So you just try not to say or show anything else,' she advised me. After the check-up, the doctor told me that I was all right, but to come back again the next day because they would like to keep a close eye on me and the baby. The doctor also told me that I should have a complete rest. At one point, I was going to ask the doctor somehow to help me, but I couldn't because Nunu's sister-in-law was with me all the time.

We all returned home very late from the hospital; I suppose it must had been about 3.30am. I was so tired and my wrist was hurting so much that I couldn't bear it any more, so I grabbed a blanket and went to the front living room, making a bed for myself on the sofa because Nunu had broken the bedroom window. I had had enough for one day, mentally and physically. I didn't have any more strength left, so I fell asleep straight away.

I'll remember that day as long as I live, because I felt so alone that it was as if I couldn't even rely on seeing my own shadow any more. I pray that no one has to go through what I went through that day. I was convinced then that I'd been born and cursed with bad luck. But, at the same time, I was 100 per cent sure that, one day, my luck would change.

The next day, I was very tired and my wrist had swollen up badly. But I had to get up and face another day. I asked Nunu's sister-in-law if there had been any news about Nunu. She told me to get ready because we were all going to visit him.

The three of us left the house in a taxi. About 15 minutes later, the taxi stopped outside a hospital called the 'Birmingham Nerve Hospital'. I asked them what kind of hospital it was, and why Nunu was there. Without giving me any other explanation, Nunu's brother just said that Nunu wasn't feeling very well, and that was why he had to be admitted to hospital.

In order to get into the building, we had to walk past two huge, securely locked doors; I was becoming even more suspicious, so I asked Nunu's sister-in-law what kind of hospital this was. Why did they have their doors locked? She said impatiently, 'That's how the hospitals are in this country!'

I thought this was very unusual; we didn't have hospitals like that in Bangladesh. A man came over to us and took us into a large, open-plan room, where there was a small group of men and women, who were all wearing the same colour clothes. I saw a few people asleep in their chairs; one woman was laughing for no reason; one man came up to me and said how beautiful I was.

Then I saw Nunu sitting in a corner watching television. We all went up to him, and I asked him what was wrong with him and what kind of hospital this was. He just looked at us and tried to speak, but I couldn't understand a word he was saying. He sounded drunk. He also looked like a completely different person to the man I saw leaving our house the day before. It didn't take me very much longer to work out exactly what sort of a place this was, and why Nunu was there. I didn't say the words 'mental hospital', but I wondered if Nunu's brother or his wife would say anything to me. But they said nothing.

After staying there for about an hour, Nunu went to sleep, so we left the hospital to return home. In the taxi, they talked about practical things, such as what to cook and bring for Nunu; they completely ignored me.

When we got back home, I just couldn't bear that treatment any more. I turned to Nunu's sister-in-law and said, 'Please, tell me what's wrong with him.'

Finally, she explained that he'd got an illness – 'manic depression' – and he'd had it since he was 15 or 16. 'He has a very serious mental illness,' she said. 'He's better most of the time, but things get worse when he doesn't take his medication. Don't worry, he'll get better soon.'

It was as though my world had suddenly been blown apart. It wasn't due to the illness, particularly, as I knew that it could happen to anybody. But why hadn't they said any of these things before he married me? Why hadn't I been told about that before and after we were married? Why hide something like that from me? They had kept me in the dark all that time. I felt completely lied to, betrayed and deceived.

I had been taken for a ride ever since Nunu's name was first mentioned by my mother's relative. It was becoming obvious to me that some of his family were particularly weird, secretive and malicious, and it's important that no one is left in any doubt that not all Bangladeshi families are like them. They are a spectacularly bad example! When they die, their bodies should be kept in a Bangladeshi museum, so they can be a warning to everyone.

Once I had found out the truth, I finally felt that at least I could deal with it, and decide how to act for the best. At least I knew what was going on. But it didn't change the fact that I was still married to Nunu, and I had my duties as a wife to consider. From then on, I made regular trips to the hospital, visiting him, taking him food, sitting and talking with him. Sometimes he would feel well enough to talk about how he felt, or he would have something to eat. On other occasions when I visited him, he was a totally different person; he just used to sit there and stare at people without saying a word. Even if I tried to feed him, he would take the food in his mouth but wouldn't eat it. It was as if he didn't know how to eat or drink, all of which was due to the medication he'd been given.

Occasionally, his brother came with me, but usually I visited him on my own. Sometimes, I used to look at the ill man sitting in front of me and reflect on how he had treated me. I just couldn't bring myself to love him, not even when he was ill and suffering. Of course, that didn't stop me from caring for him and looking after him, which is something I would have done for any patient with a mental illness. By the time Nunu had been there for a week, the doctor said that within a few days he could come home.

I still felt quite shocked at everything that had happened, and now I was going to have to prepare myself for Nunu's return. After thinking about this long and hard over the next few days, and fully aware of the possible consequences, I decided to tell my family everything about how we had all been deceived by Nunu's family.

That day, I wrote a letter to my father and put that under my pillow, so I could post it the next day. The same day, at about 5.30pm, I went to the hospital with some food to see Nunu. When I arrived, I noticed that he seemed different somehow. I sat next to him and offered him the food I had brought, but he didn't want to eat anything. Instead, he had a go at me for bringing the food without asking him!

After he'd finished telling me off, he told me that his doctor had told him that he was completely better and that he was allowed to go home whenever he wanted. So he got up and walked out, with me following in his wake. Once out of the hospital, he called a taxi and we left.

In the taxi, he told me that he wasn't going to go back to his brother's house in Birmingham. 'Where do you want to go then?' I asked nervously.

'I want to go to my other brother's house in Newcastle,' he replied. 'There's a better hospital there; I've always gone to that hospital whenever I've been ill.'

'We couldn't go just like that,' I pleaded with him. 'Let's go home and discuss this with your brother. Then we can go if you want. And, anyway, we've got all our clothes there ... I've got nothing with me.'

He told me to be quiet, as he had made up his mind. There was no way he was going to stop that taxi. So we left Birmingham, and all sorts of worries started racing through my mind. I knew very well that, as soon as they found out about this back at the house, there would be hell to pay as far as I was concerned. I was also nervous about going to Newcastle to live with another new family whom I had never even met ... and who didn't know we were coming!

Things were pretty bad already but, to make matters worse, Nunu told me that he didn't even have the taxi fare for the journey! I couldn't believe that we were, by now, on the motorway without either of us having a penny in our pockets! Nunu said he wasn't worried, as his other brother would pay when we arrived. I didn't have sufficient strength or courage to reason with him any more; I just fell asleep.

After a long journey, we finally arrived in Newcastle, in an area called Jesmond. His brother paid the £100 taxi fare, but I received a lecture for being an irresponsible wife. His wife was nice to me, though, and things appeared a little more hopeful as they also had two girls about eleven or twelve years old and a boy, who was about seven.

After having a rest, I rang Birmingham to explain to them exactly what had happened. They were seething with anger when they heard the full story, and weren't even prepared to listen to me, immediately blaming me for not having stopped Nunu from leaving the hospital. I apologised, because I should have checked with the doctors, but was it really my fault that I couldn't speak English? I was so tired and fed up I just went to bed ... after all, I was still heavily pregnant.

Just as I was about to fall asleep, Nunu woke me up, saying that he wasn't feeling very well. I woke his brother up, told him how Nunu was feeling, and he then talked to Nunu for a while. Eventually, Nunu was admitted to a mental institution called the St Nicholas Hospital in Newcastle. I couldn't sleep at all that night, and was left wondering about how the day had gone from bad to worse ... and then had just lurched into truly awful.

I'll never forget how I felt that night; it seemed as though I was slowly drifting into an impenetrable darkness that might stop me from ever seeing the light again. I strongly believed that, if I had loved Nunu, none of those problems would have mattered to me. I'm Bangladeshi, and I can survive anything in life that's thrown at me – that's a fact. In dealing with my current situation, love would have been my greatest source of strength.

A few days later, as another chapter of my life began in Newcastle, I phoned Birmingham to organise for our clothes to be sent up to us. Nunu's brother picked up the phone, and the moment he heard my voice he started being extremely insulting towards me. He called me the most dreadful names, which shocked me, but I didn't have a clue what I had done wrong this time.

It turned out that the letter I had written to my father in Bangladesh about Nunu's illness had been found by his wife. She had discovered it under my pillow in my room and decided to read it out to her husband. That was the last thing I needed! I didn't know what to say to defend myself and, despite him being a couple of hundred miles away, I was becoming more and more worried by Nunu's brother's behaviour. He had even found out that I used to talk to the man who lived opposite their house.

Nunu's brother wasn't prepared to listen to what I had to say; although I tried for two weeks to make him see sense, nothing worked. By then, though, I had started to get used to being blamed by him for everything. That made me feel a little sad, as I had respected him and had looked up to him as an older brother.

Three weeks later, they sent us our clothes through a family friend. I was back in my usual routine again by then, visiting Nunu in the hospital every day, taking food for him and sitting there talking to him, helping him to get better. I even made a few friends with some of the patients there. One old lady used to say hello to me all the time. Another patient was Tony; I can still remember him. Every time

I met him he would come up to me and give me a kiss on my hand, and then he offered to teach me English. He was really funny, and used to make me laugh. With Nunu's permission, sometimes he used to touch my belly to feel the baby. The strange thing was, he didn't seem to look ill. He always had a warm, affectionate look in his eyes, and I was really good at sizing people up when I was able to study their faces; I never make any mistakes when I read people's eyes.

One day, though, I went to visit Nunu as usual, but I couldn't see Tony anywhere. So I asked Nunu where Tony was. 'Look in that corner,' he said. So I looked over to where Nunu was pointing, and I saw Tony sitting in a chair and staring at the television, dribbling like a child. Obviously, he was on some sort of medication. I'll always remember that, after a while, when he noticed me, he got up with the help of the nurse. Tony couldn't walk properly but shuffled over and, even in that state, he insisted on kissing my hand. He looked at me, smiled, then shuffled away.

That day, I came home, locked myself in my room and broke down in tears. It was amazing that Tony was so ill, but still felt it was important to say hello to me. I found that really touching.

I never saw Tony again after that. God bless him, wherever he is. Sometimes, throughout your life, you meet some people and, before you know it, they touch your heart. Their impact on you always stays with you, no matter what.

By now, I was getting closer to the due date for giving birth. The atmosphere in the house wasn't helping me a great deal, though. Everyone blamed me for not helping Nunu to overcome his illness; after all, that was the reason they'd got him married off to me. But how on earth did they think I could cure Nunu's severe mental illness? I'm not a bloody psychiatrist! That is just typical of the stupidity that surrounded me on a daily basis.

Despite all this, I was doing my best to survive. One of the most uncomfortable situations was what I had to eat in their house. Even though they were well off financially – they had their own restaurant business – nearly every day I was given chicken curry and rice. There was little else. I was sick of eating the same thing every day, and it worried me that I wasn't eating any of the recommended foods that pregnant women should have for a balanced diet. I couldn't ask for anything else, because I was too embarrassed to ask for things; my background prevented me. Being pregnant, though, I was always hungry. The hardest thing for me was waking up hungry in the middle of the night, but there would be nothing in the kitchen to eat; sometimes I would just help myself to some fruit, whenever there was some around.

One day, I went to bed early, at around 9.30pm. I was just lying on the bed trying to sleep, when I heard Nunu's sister-in-law talking on the phone to the other sister-in-law in Birmingham. She was saying, 'I couldn't believe Nunu's wife eats all the fruit at night when she's hungry and, in the morning, there's not much left for the children's packed lunches.'

Naturally, when I heard that I was very hurt, as I'm very sensitive. I lay back on the bed and cried until I fell asleep. I felt disgusted with them, hardly able to believe that they would say such things about a pregnant woman. And what a bitch for even thinking that, let alone saying it! Instead of looking after me as the older sister-in-law, as tradition would suggest, she was stabbing me in the back, all over some pathetic bits of fruit! I'll never forget that as long as I live.

From that day, I never went to their kitchen at night to eat anything, no matter how hungry I was. I can be very stubborn at times if I want to be. I used to bring a glass of water up to my room, but that was all. There were many nights when I just made do with what I had, as I preferred to go without any food rather than listen to all those hurtful comments.

Visiting Nunu at the hospital was something else I hated. And the worst part of it was that Nunu was allowed to spend some time with me in privacy. Now, he knew very well that I was heavily pregnant, but he still insisted on treating me as though I was an object for his personal use, only because I was his wife. He didn't have any respect for me whatsoever, and he never cared that I was heavily pregnant. Suffice it to say, that it was like I was being raped, and I was not in a fit condition to endure some of his demands. And why the hell should I? What a sick man he was; I suppose I should be grateful he was kept at the hospital, and wasn't torturing me constantly at home.

After a while, I couldn't tolerate it any longer. I had to stop him abusing me like that. One day, after my usual visit, I was waiting for a taxi outside the hospital. One of the nurses from that unit was walking by, and when he saw me he came and sat down next to me. He asked me if was all right, as I looked a little bit upset.

Without answering his question, I broke down in tears. He realised that something was wrong, so he just put his arm around me to comfort me. He knew that I couldn't speak or understand English, so he wasn't sure how to communicate with me. I realised that, somehow, I'd got to tell him that I didn't want to be alone with Nunu any more when I was visiting him.

Painstakingly, in broken English, I told the nurse that, whenever Nunu was with me alone, he was using me to satisfy his lust. I felt used and abused. He didn't even care that I was heavily pregnant! I couldn't go through any more pain. I finally begged him, 'Please help me … or I'll just finish my life!'

Believe me, that took me a good 20 minutes at least to get my point across to the nurse, who listened and encouraged me to tell him exactly how I felt, and what I wanted.

I was lucky that the nurse managed to understand what was happening. From that moment on, the nurse made sure somehow that I was never left alone with Nunu. I was very grateful to him for that. It's sad that I never got to know his name, but I'll always be grateful to him for being so kind to me, and helping me out. It was also reassuring to know that some kind men do exist. It was a little bit of comfort that meant so much to me. He must have been God-sent that day.

7 BORN AGAIN

During the last few weeks of my pregnancy, I became a very different person. I regularly sat in my room and cried for fear of giving birth. Often, at night, I used to look out through the window and imagine ripping away every silent, painful moment of my life and capturing some happiness. But, as I had come to expect, destiny had something else planned for me. Any ray of happiness was still just beyond my grasp.

As normal, I went to bed one evening and, in the middle of the night, I started to have severe pains. The pain came and went all night, along with a pain in my back as well. I didn't want to wake anyone in the house but, at about 6.30 in the morning, I couldn't wait any longer. So I knocked on Nunu's sister-in law's door.

Nunu's brother took me to the hospital; I was petrified because everything that was about to happen was new to me. He left me in the hospital on my own, because in our culture a brother-in-law would not normally stay with a woman in labour. And, anyway, some men don't like being there for the birth; they leave that to the women, as they believe it's very much an event to be shared with other women. I personally think that the father should be with the mother, no matter what the circumstances; but if he's too weak to cope, or if he faints at the sight of blood, that's a different matter!

I knew that at least I could rely on my hospital interpreter being with me; her name was Mrs Mondol. She was a very nice lady and, whenever I met her at the hospital when I went along for a check-up, she used to make me feel much more comfortable.

Shortly after I was admitted to the maternity unit, she came to see me. I was relieved to see her because, much of the time, I couldn't communicate with the nurses. She stayed with me for most of the day before she had to leave but, before her shift ended, she asked the hospital social worker, Lisa Brazier, to keep an eye on me for a while. She was another wonderful lady.

My pain was becoming much worse by this time. The doctor told me that the baby wasn't due for another two days at least. They said I could go home and rest there if I wanted, but I told them that there was no one there to care for me, so could I stay in the hospital for the next two days? I felt pathetic when I made that request, but I just didn't want to go back home. At least in the hospital the nurses would care for me. Fortunately, God must have been smiling on me then, because they were kind enough to let me stay. I'll never forget their kindness.

At night, the back pain grew even worse, so to ease the pain I was given a very strong injection. Eventually, I fell asleep, but it was a fitful sleep. I had my recurring dream about the same mystery man, the same dream I had had when I was in Bangladesh. I can still remember that dream very clearly; he was sitting beside me, holding my hand. He helped me get up from bed, as he stood in front of me. I was looking at him, touching his face. He smiled, and with his smile the whole room lit up. Without saying anything he went behind me and cuddled up to me; I could feel his heartbeat on my back. His hands on my belly made all my pain disappear. I felt very peaceful from within.

I just couldn't believe that dream. It's beyond my understanding!

Even in that condition my mind played tricks with me, otherwise what else would you call it? I can't explain why I keep on having this dream. Who is he and why does he come into my dreams. Especially when I've been in very sad situations. I woke up, but I was alone. The pain was a little bit better than before, and then the nurse came to my bed to let me know that Nunu had rung, and that he'd see me the next day. Shortly after that, some of Nunu's family came to see me for a while, but they didn't even bring me a great deal of food. Then again, I wasn't disappointed, because I never expected any consideration from them anyway.

On the second day, Mrs Mondol visited me as well, and that was nice. Shortly afterwards, Nunu came to see me for a little while. I didn't want him anywhere near me. I was getting sick of the way he behaved. But, sometimes, I felt that I had to be nice to him, as I simply didn't know whether he would suddenly become violent towards me.

That night, I was standing by the hospital window watching other pregnant women coming to the hospital with their husbands and families. I thought to myself that they were so lucky, and there I was in my room all on my own. I was missing my family in Bangladesh terribly; I wished they were with me. And I wondered what it would feel like to have a loving husband who would sit with me and hold me close to him. Standing by the window, a few hot tears stung my eyes. I just wanted the long night to end.

It wasn't long before the pain started again. I was crying in agony, so the nurse came in and gave me some painkillers. Later on, a male nurse came to check up on my condition, but he didn't have to ask me how I was. He could see for himself how distressed I was, not only coping with the pain but also the fact of being alone. I looked at him, hoping he'd make everything better. The nurse just held my hand and said, 'Everything will be all right ... don't worry.' Before he left the room, he asked me if I wanted anything. I felt like saying,

'Yes, a hug, please!' But I couldn't say anything. In actual fact, all I wanted was somebody to hold me close to him, and reassure me that he was there for me. Silently, I was crying out for some love and affection, but I never let anyone see that.

On 19 January 1991, after three days and a nightmare of pain, I gave birth to a beautiful baby daughter. And all my pain went away! I had a normal delivery, and all my physical and mental distress dissolved as soon as I saw her tiny little face. What a wonderful feeling, holding your own baby in your arms. She was a little part of me. I cocooned her in my lap, looking at her tiny face, and said to myself, 'From today, I'll dedicate all my life to you.' It was truly the happiest day of my life; I was thrilled to bits!

Nunu's mother said to me that she wished I'd given birth to a boy instead of a girl. She added that, given Nunu's condition, having a son would have helped him. I asked her how she could say that while holding my newborn baby in her arms. The reason she wanted a boy for her son, of course, is because in our culture boys are seen to represent stability and a future for their parents, unlike the girls in the family, who have to get married and start a new family somewhere else.

From then on, whenever any of Nunu's relatives heard the news of my perfect little daughter, they used to feel sorry for me for having had a girl. But I never let any of that nonsense get to me; I was too busy enjoying my little baby in my life.

A few hours later, Nunu's entire family came to see the baby. I wondered where Nunu was, but then I realised that it was night-time, so the hospital might not have allowed him to leave. I had a good night's rest everything considered; the nurse put my baby next to me. Throughout the night when I wasn't sleeping, I was looking at my baby, admiring her, looking at her tiny little hands and feet. I just couldn't resist checking up on her every five minutes to see if she was all right.

The next day, in the morning, my social worker Lisa and Mrs Mondol came to see us, and Lisa kindly gave me some second-hand clothes for my baby. I wasn't complaining, but I couldn't believe that Nunu's family hadn't even bought the newest addition to their family some brand-new clothes of her own.

My newborn baby had to wear second-hand clothes as her first outfit. I know it might not be a big issue in Western culture, but, in Bangladesh, we buy the newborn baby new clothes for the moment they are born. I believe any mother would understand. I'll never forget that. I thanked Lisa, anyway, and put the clothes on my baby, trying not to let my tears show.

At around midday, I asked Mrs Mondol where Nunu was, as he hadn't even been to see the baby yet. She didn't answer my question directly but, instead, she said, 'We all need to talk to you about certain things … about Nunu … later on in a meeting.'

I started to suspect that something wasn't right, but I didn't know then that I was in for the most dreadful shock.

Lisa and Mrs Mondol returned to the room with a cup of tea for me. They both held my hands and said that they needed to tell me some bad news, that it might be a little bit of a shock, but that they were there to help me. Both of them were trying to soften the blow and comfort me as much as they could before they even told me what the bad news was. I said, 'I'm sorry, but none of this is making any sense! Just tell me what has happened.'

Lisa asked the nurse to look after the baby and then, as Lisa was speaking, Mrs Mondol interpreted what she said for me in Bengali. Lisa tried to keep it brief: 'Before Nunu went to Bangladesh to get married to you, it was discovered that he constituted a potential threat to young children. So, from now on, whenever he wants to see the baby, there will be someone from the social services present. That is the reason Nunu hasn't been to see the baby, because we had to organise a supervised visit.'

I was speechless. For a moment, I thought I was having a bad dream and that, as soon as I woke up, everything would be back to normal. I asked Mrs Mondol if the date was 1 April, because, if that had been an April Fool's joke, I didn't find it very funny. They reassured me that it wasn't any sort of joke, but the truth. I didn't know what to feel. All I can remember is asking Lisa to give me a hug and hold me tight. I was so angry, and I wanted to cry but I didn't have any tears left. I felt empty.

It took them a while to explain to me what the situation would mean, as I had never heard of anything like it while I was in Bangladesh.

After a while, they took me with them into the more formal meeting, where we all had to discuss the matter with various agencies – the child protection team, Nunu's social worker, the hospital's doctor and also Nunu's brother; of course, Lisa and Mrs Mondol were with me as well. I walked into the room and sat down, looking straight into Nunu's brother's eyes. I could feel the anger inside me building up slowly like a volcano, but I kept quiet and said nothing, just listening to what Mrs Mondol was interpreting.

But I couldn't keep my cool for very long. I lost my temper and burst into tears at the same time, and focused my anger on Nunu's brother. 'Why have you destroyed my life? My whole marriage is based on one big lie! Now my daughter's life is affected as well. Why didn't you say anything before you married him off to me? What right do you have to torture me like that?'

I thought to myself, 'What a lie, what a way to deceive me. How many more shocks do I have to endure?' The fact remained that they had lied to my family and me before our marriage. What could be more evil than that? What had I ever done to deserve that? As far as I knew, I'd always tried to be a decent person for everyone's benefit. Then why did it happen to me?

I must admit, that day I lost faith in everything for a while. My whole marriage was based on one enormous lie. I felt as though I had lost the strength to fight, but I wasn't on my own any more – I had my little baby to think about.

After the meeting, Lisa took me back to my room and brought my baby back to me. I held her in my arms and said, 'From today, I'll be your mother as well as your father and, as far as Nunu is concerned, he can go to hell, and I mean pure, burning hell.' I didn't want him anywhere near her. Unfortunately, the fact was that he was her biological father … but that's all he was. She was *my* daughter. End of story.

Later on that day, Nunu did come to see my baby with his social worker. I didn't want him to, but legally I couldn't stop him. It struck me how strange the system of law was in England – allowing someone with his history to see a child, just because he happens to be her biological father. Looking at Nunu holding my baby, I felt sick. I just knew that I wouldn't be able to trust Nunu with her at all. For the next few hours, I was in no frame of mind to talk to anyone. I had to make a decision about my deceitful marriage, and I had to think about my baby as well.

Taking stock of the situation, there didn't seem to be very much going for me: I was in a country where I had no family or relatives to support me; I couldn't communicate with anybody in English; within 12 hours of giving birth to a child, I had found out that the man I was married was a potential danger to children. My circumstances couldn't possibly have got any worse! But I hadn't lost yet; I had to continue to fight to protect my innocent baby. I had to wipe all my tears for her sake, as I was her mother now.

It was particularly difficult for me in the maternity unit, because there were three other mothers there as well with their babies. I would watch their husbands and families coming to take them home. I would never experience that.

After a lot of thinking, I made a final decision – divorce. Even if I had wanted to carry on living with Nunu, the social services and the child protection team wouldn't have allowed that, as I'd have my baby living with me in the house as well. My number-one priority from that moment was to protect my little baby.

Then, the next morning, when Lisa and Mrs Mondol arrived, I asked them if they could arrange for me to stay in the hospital for an extra few days. I really didn't want to go back to Nunu's brother's house. The hospital was kind enough to let me stay there for a few more days, and from that day on I started to take control of my own life, as well as my daughter's.

Then the time came for me to let my family know what was happening to me. I had no money, so I asked Mrs Mondol if she could find a way for me to phone Bangladesh, and Lisa was very kind, letting me use the telephone in her office.

My family were delighted to hear about my daughter, but then I told my father the full story of everything that had happened ... and everything that had been discovered. He was so shocked that he went very quiet for a few seconds. Then, in a tearful voice, he said, 'Listen, you're my daughter, you have to be strong. I'm always with you.'

He was pleased that Lisa and Mrs Mondol were there to help me, and then I told him that I couldn't spend the rest of my life with someone like Nunu. I was stunned at his reply: 'Why haven't you left him yet?'

That gave me all the confidence I needed. The rest of my family agreed with my father, and I think they realised what a mistake they'd made. My father told me that he regretted ever having allowed my marriage to Nunu to go ahead, and he seemed to feel so guilty that I was worried about his health.

After I put the phone down, I felt reborn. That was it! I didn't have to waste any more time sitting and thinking – I asked for a solicitor, so I could start the divorce proceedings immediately. I felt good, as well. I believe that, under similar circumstances, other women may have simply been crushed. I don't know how I managed to keep my sanity, but I did. I simply followed my instinct. I tried my very best to focus on the positive side of things, even though it took an enormous effort of will. Later on, my Sami's name had to remain a 'ward of court' for her own protection. I was very pleased with that because I knew that at least that way she would be safe. I'll always be grateful to the court for protecting my daughter that way.

When Nunu and his family heard what I had decided to do, they thought that I had lost my mind. Nunu's mother said, 'No other man will ever marry you … decent men don't marry a divorcée. And they won't accept your daughter, either. You should sacrifice your life to Nunu … you're a Bangladeshi woman!'

After letting her get all her nonsense off her chest, for the first time I stood up to her. 'Shut up,' I said, 'and get out of my sight! I've got no place in my life for people like you!'

After staying in the hospital for a further week, Lisa found me a place in a women's refuge. I must admit, after hearing all about the refuge, I felt uncomfortable going there. Besides, I didn't want to take my newborn baby to a refuge instead of a home. So I discussed that with Mrs Mondol and Lisa, and they both said that they would help me to find my own place to live. In the meantime, I decided to go back to Nunu's brother's house until something came up.

So I returned to the house in Jesmond, which had become even more like hell on earth. I just ignored all the constant nagging at me; I was expecting that. My father always taught me, 'Do not lower yourself to people who try to pull you down to their level, because you'll always be a step above them.' That was hard to put into practice, though!

I had some nice letters from my family in Bangladesh, and they even suggested a few names for my daughter – I chose 'Sami'. I thought that was the cutest name of the lot. She was such an adorable baby when she was tiny … and she still is!

A few weeks later, I had a letter from my brother saying that my father had become quite ill after hearing how Nunu was a potential threat to children. My father wrote to me all the time, telling me to get out of the marriage as soon as possible. He was particularly worried for Sami.

Nunu was still an in-patient at the mental hospital, but he used to come to the house with his social worker to see Sami. I hated him for having any contact with her, but legally I couldn't do much to stop him. It made me feel sick seeing him with her. I have to admit he was all right with her, but I could tell in his attitude that, just like his mother, he had wanted a son instead of a daughter. To my mind, someone like him doesn't deserve to have any children at all, boy or girl.

8 A NEW START

I was delighted. Lisa had found me a house in the West End of Newcastle. What would I have done without Lisa? I'll appreciate everything that lady has done for me all my life. At times, she was more like a mother to me rather than a social worker. She also found me a good solicitor in Newcastle in order to start the divorce proceedings.

I went to see the house for the first time with Lisa, taking Sami as well. I took my little Sami everywhere I went, and was perhaps a little overprotective towards her. I am even now, but I suppose it's hardly surprising given what I've been through. I liked the house, and told Nunu's family that I was moving out. They knew very well that social services were involved, and I think that's the reason they didn't try to stop me.

I moved into the new house with Sami, and we were very happy there, even though there was nothing in the house except an old bed. One precious thing I did have at that time, though, was my peace of mind. Lisa also sorted out some finance for me through the social security benefit. I hated resorting to charity, but what choice did I have? Sometimes, I couldn't help feeling a little ashamed that I had to live on social security. Lisa tried to make me feel better by saying that it was my legal right to claim benefit; it wasn't charity. But I still felt humiliated. I found it hard to believe that my father had once been a rich man in Bangladesh. We used to give away so much money and clothing every month, and now I was the same daughter who had to live on charity. Fate can be terribly cruel.

I can still remember Sami and I always bought second-hand clothes, bedding, cooking utensils and so on. One horrible incident I'll never forget. As usual I put Sami in her pram and went along to a second-hand shop. I picked up a top for Sami and asked the shopkeeper for the size of something. Obviously the shopkeeper didn't understand my broken English and became very annoyed; he actually threw me out of the shop. I didn't even understand all the swear words he was using on me. But now I do. He said he was sick and tired of all the 'Pakis' in his country.

Nunu's family didn't help me at all. My English next-door neighbour brought me blankets and other essential items, and a Bangladeshi lady brought me home-cooked Bangladeshi food for three days until I had bought a cooker. I had to accept that because I had no other alternative. Those people who helped me were strangers at first, only my neighbours, but they showed me far more humanity and kindness than I had ever received from my husband's family.

Although things were generally more positive for me and Sami now, from time to time, I wished I could show someone just how much pain was locked away in my heart. We were in a new house, in a new area, so I felt a little bit frightened at first, but I soon got used to that. The most important thing was that I was suddenly free. There was no pressure from anyone, no one to give me any hassle. I didn't have to justify anything to anyone. Finally, things had started to look up for my daughter and me. I suppose I should have seen the dark clouds forming … it wasn't long before the 'mother-in-law from hell' had to spoil it all, by deciding to move in with me.

When I heard that that was what she wanted to do, I told Nunu to tell his mother that I didn't want her in my house; I could manage on my own. But then Nunu started to play his psychological games. He said that, if I moved into a house on my own, some people in our own community would think very badly of me. Without a husband, I'd have no respect in society. People would start to think I might be seeing other men. And there was the gossip to think about as well. 'Do you want people to give you a bad name?' he asked.

I have to admit, he managed to get me to accept that some of this was true – people would gossip about a single woman living on her own. But I had bargained for that when I decided to move out to my own house.

Unfortunately, I ended up agreeing with much of what he said, and he managed to get me to agree to his mother moving in, although I understood that it would only be for a short while. Deep down, I knew the real reason she moved in. She was aware that I was planning to leave Nunu, so she thought that if she moved in with me she could persuade me to change my mind.

I kept in touch with my family in Bangladesh on the telephone. They were proud of the way I was handling Sami's life and mine, especially my father. I instinctively knew that my father wasn't going to be with us for much longer. The nightmare of my life had affected him severely; after all, I was his only daughter. Since I had married Nunu, everything had gone from bad to worse for my family in Bangladesh. Our financial situation wasn't improving, and my father was extremely worried about my brother Raj and his future. I felt as though my entire family was falling apart. I promised myself that, whatever it took, I would pull my family back together, regardless of what was happening in my own life.

The first thing that I needed to focus on now was the divorce. I said to Lisa that I needed to see my solicitor, David, as soon as possible, so she organised a meeting with him. The following week, I met David and started the divorce proceedings. Oh, how good that felt! It was the best decision I'd ever made! I liked David, who was very kind and generous. He had worked with a lot of Asian people, and had even visited Bangladesh. Again, it was comforting to know that there were some decent people around who were prepared to help when needed.

Although that made me feel really good about myself, there was still the situation surrounding Nunu's visits that had to be sorted out. Nunu was still allowed to visit my Sami twice a week under the supervision of the social services. One day, Nunu came to see Sami while his mother was in the house as well. I was in the kitchen making a cup of tea for myself, when Nunu joined me in the kitchen with his mother. He said, 'Come on, why are you talking about a divorce? We could sort out things between ourselves.'

I said nothing.

Then he said, 'Why don't you give Sami to the social services for a few weeks? Then I could stay in the house ...'

That was it! It was one of the most outrageous suggestions I'd ever heard. He couldn't have pushed me any further! I'd managed a certain amount of self-control up to this point, but then I lost it – big time! I pushed him out of the kitchen, shouting, 'Give Sami to the social services? Over my dead body! Get the hell out of my house and my life.'

Then his social worker came into the kitchen to calm the situation down, but nothing could stop me. I just went crazy. I looked around for something suitable to hit him with, but his mother and the social worker stopped me somehow. He was lucky, because any other woman would have had his balls for earrings for suggesting that!

How could he say something like that about my Sami? Who the hell did he think he was? As I threw him out of my house, I heard him muttering that, because of Sami, he wasn't allowed to live in the house. I said, 'You're a pervert, so you shouldn't be anywhere near Sami or me.' It showed perfectly just how perverted Nunu could be at times – asking me to give up my daughter so he could play at happy families! Think again!

His mother was very angry with me after that, and started to give me a lecture about how I should be ashamed of myself, that I wasn't fit to be his wife. She cursed me and said, 'I hope you die and go to hell!' Then she said in a patronising tone that I had shamed Bangladeshi culture, and that Nunu should have given me a good beating … only then would I have stayed under control.

I tried to talk to her to reach some sort of understanding, but it didn't work. Now, I'm not the sort of person who would choose to be disrespectful to someone older, but she was more than just an older relative – she was an evil witch who had just wished me dead, so normal rules simply didn't apply in this case. Having lost all respect for her, I went upstairs to her room, grabbed all her belongings and threw them out of the window. I shouted, 'Get out of my house, or I might do something I'll regret!' I don't know what came over me. At first, she refused to leave, then she rang her older son and asked him to pick her up. I felt strong and in control – and it was a feeling I really enjoyed.

After she'd left, I felt great, made a cup of tea and sat down with my baby. I was ready to face anything; all I had to do was believe in myself. There was nothing to stop me moving forwards now; there was no one to dictate what I should or shouldn't do any longer, so I could just get on with building a life for my daughter and myself. I couldn't forget how unfortunate I had been up to this point in my life, but, if I ever got married again, I resolved to make sure that it was to someone who didn't have any other relatives at all! If all in-laws turned out to be like Nunu's, then who needs them? I couldn't go through all that pain, manipulation and deceit again. Fortunately, there were some isolated shafts of light in the general gloom – several special people had helped me enormously in the past, and I was sure that there would be others in the future. I felt quietly confident that I'd find my perfect match one day.

Gradually, I started to speak English, although I still needed to improve a great deal. I asked Lisa to help me to find a college; I wanted to study English and possibly get on to some sort of course, so I would be in a better position to get a job at some point.

Lisa took me to Newcastle College, where I got a place on a part-time English course, and she found me a nursery for Sami. I felt really good about myself, and a great deal more confident. It was such a relief knowing that I didn't have to cover myself up from head to toe any longer, and I changed my image, sometimes wearing Western clothes in college. I also managed to make some really good friends.

Some Asian people admired my bravery, while others hated me for changing my appearance and lifestyle so drastically. Some even said I was becoming more like a young English woman, that I was adopting their culture. How could I become English when I'd been born and brought up in Bangladesh? My culture and values are in my heart and soul, not in the clothes I choose to wear. I hadn't changed inwardly at all!

I must admit that I never had any hassle from anyone from the English community. But, even if I had, I was past caring about what other people thought of me. I grew to believe that, if someone talked ill of me, I wasn't going to retaliate and descend to their level. I was simply going to continue doing what I thought was right for me and my daughter and, if that bothered someone, too bad! As long as no harm came to Sami or me, I did what I felt had to be done. I had realised that I only have to answer to myself for my actions while I'm alive, nobody else.

I believed that, if I put 100 per cent effort into something, I could never fail. From the moment I had Sami, and stood up to Nunu's vindictive relatives, I've never doubted myself. My little Sami gave me a massive amount of strength to move on. At the same time, I knew I would have many more hurdles and hardship to overcome. But I had a great deal of self-belief, and I didn't have any intention of letting that weaken.

Lisa was still involved in helping me, but not as much as she had been. The reason for this was because I could manage for most of the time on my own. My little Sami was now six months old; she was my number-one priority and always will be. During that time, I had managed to stop Nunu from seeing Sami, so I hadn't heard a thing from Nunu or his family for six months. I was beginning to feel relieved that his days of harassing us were over.

But I'd spoken too soon. One day, he turned up on my doorstep, demanding to see his daughter. I didn't let him in, but then he started to kick at the door. I became quite frightened, and ended up calling the police but, sadly, he'd disappeared by the time they arrived.

He returned on several subsequent occasions. Meanwhile, my solicitor wrote to his solicitor to order him to stay away from us. That didn't work, as his family started to send other people to see me to try to talk me into calling off the divorce. Eventually, I was left with no option but to call the police whenever someone came to call on Nunu's behalf.

Another of Nunu's relatives who lived in the same city as us in Bangladesh, started to give my family a hard time as well. He threatened me by saying that, if I ever went back to Bangladesh, they'd take my Sami away from me by law. Much as I didn't want to, I had to take that threat 100 per cent seriously, and I still do, because I know that Nunu and his scheming family would do anything to take my Sami away from me. Don't forget, I had lived with them, so I knew exactly what they were capable of doing.

Sami is everything to me and, naturally, I would do anything to protect her. I therefore had to make a very painful decision – I wouldn't go to Bangladesh until Sami reached 16. That way, at least, I could make sure that she was protected. I admit, I'm an overprotective mother ... but there was no way I would take any risk with her livelihood.

A year later, I passed my English course at the college. As a result, I decided to take up another course, an access to higher education. I was really enjoying my college life, and I was determined to achieve something.

I kept myself busy with my regular routine, but deep down I was very lonely. Despite what Nunu had put me through, I never gave up the hope that I'd find a man one day who would love me more than anything else. While I longed for love and companionship, I suppose it was inevitable that I fell for someone who was showing me a great deal of kindness and respect at that time – my solicitor, David. I knew it wasn't love, and that I was probably just responding to him being a really caring, decent person, with no sexual undertones or impropriety on his part, so I guess it was silly of me. But I had such a desire for love and affection that I forgot he was only doing his job.

The embarrassing thing was that I told him how I felt. But even here he was kind and considerate, and tried not to make me feel uncomfortable. And, gently, he told me he was married. Well, that came as a bit of a shock! When I realised that I shouldn't be feeling that way towards him, I decided to regard him as nothing but my solicitor which indeed had always been the true position. He'll always remain, as far as I'm concerned, the best solicitor on earth. In a way, it proved to me that my personal trauma had not affected my hope and belief that, one day, I would enjoy my own perfect relationship.

Another year passed, and it wasn't long before I'd graduate from college, and then I'd be able to start looking for a job. Once I'd got that, I'd not only be able to look after Sami and myself, but I could also support my family in Bangladesh at the same time. Occasionally, I felt really useless not being able to help them, but how could I in my circumstances? It made me feel very guilty, sometimes to the point of not being able to eat, as I thought of my elderly father, and whether he had enough food in the house. I wondered how my little baby brother Joynal was coping, and I imagined my mother's sad face as I sat down at my own dinner table. There were many nights when I went to sleep without eating; I just couldn't help it.

Most of the time, I was worried about my father, as he was very ill. His condition had progressively deteriorated for a number of reasons, but I believed the main cause to be my situation regarding Nunu and his family. My father was heartbroken because I wasn't happily married. I hold Nunu and his family fully responsible for my father's condition; they were bad news from day one!

The situation was so bad that my family didn't even have enough money to take my father to the hospital for special treatment. I knew that I had to do something, I couldn't just sit back and watch my father suffering. But I knew very well that, until I got some sort of qualification, nobody would offer me a job with good pay.

Finally, as a last resort, I decided to contact some old friends of my family from Bangladesh who had lived for many years in London, whom I didn't really know but who I'd heard were very well off. So I went to them and asked for a large loan, and promised them that I would personally pay them back when I could afford to in a few years' time. If not, then I'd sort it out later from Bangladesh when we got back on track.

After hearing all the details of our family's problems, they were kind enough to give me the loan, so, along with contributions from my cousin in America and a few close friends in England, I managed to raise around £15,000. That was enough to start helping my family to turn things around. I just had to do something to help my family; I would even have sold my own blood to help them, and they knew it, too. I had the family friends and my cousin send all the money directly to Bangladesh.

The main priority was to get my father admitted to a good hospital for the best possible treatment, and I was able to provide that for him. Then I asked my mum to give some of the remaining money to my brother Raj, and asked him to consider going abroad to get a job and reorganise his life, as he hadn't had any luck in Bangladesh. He turned out to be very lucky – within a few months, he'd got his visa for America, where my cousin and his family were prepared to help him settle down. I was so pleased with that result.

Then, with what little I had left, my family bought back some of the land we'd lost because of the business. Finally, things started to look up and, when my family established themselves, they wanted to pay back the loan, but I insisted on paying the loan myself instead. So I asked my mother to sell some of the land that I was going to inherit later on. It seemed the most obvious thing to do, really. I'd never need land … all I needed was love.

9 PROFIT ... AND LOSS

I should have learned by now ... when things are going well for us, a storm is probably brewing, ready to sweep everything away. Only two weeks before my brother was going to leave Bangladesh, I rang our house. I usually spoke to everyone when I rang, but that particular day, when I asked to speak to my father, my brother told me that he wasn't feeling very well. I don't know why, but I had a very bad feeling deep down that they were hiding something from me. From then on, I stopped going to college for a while; I couldn't eat properly, and I couldn't concentrate on anything that I was doing. I also noticed that, for a couple of weeks, I hadn't received any letters from my father.

Four days went by, and then I rang Bangladesh again to check if my father was feeling any better. Again, they said that my father wasn't feeling well enough to come to the phone. For some strange reason, my mother and brothers were unusually nice to me. I suspected strongly that there was something terribly wrong with my father. That evening, my next-door neighbour Linda and another family friend, Mr Miah, came to see me. I was pleased to see them; I told them that, for the last few days, I had been extremely worried about my father.

Then the two of them started to act strangely as well. Linda offered to make me a cup of tea and Mr Miah started cooking for me in the kitchen, which was normally something I would do when guests arrived. I let this pass for the time being, and we all had something to eat. By that time, it was 9.30pm. I put Sami to bed and, when I came back down, Linda and Mr Miah sat next to me. Linda gave me a hug and said, 'You know how you've been having strange feelings about your father? Well, I'm so sorry to say that you were right ... your father died three days ago. Mr Miah had a call from your brothers in Bangladesh. The reason your family told us to come and tell you in person was because they wanted us to be here for you.'

Slowly, quietly, I asked Linda to repeat everything she'd said. She did. I felt that my whole world had just fallen apart. My father was my biggest strength and he'd left me. I told Linda and Mr Miah that that couldn't be right, they must have made some sort of mistake, because my father had promised me that he would be waiting for me at the coach station when I returned to Bangladesh. Gently, they reassured me that they were telling me the truth.

I was in a state of total shock. I didn't know what to feel or what to do. I just wanted somebody to tell me that it wasn't true. I knew my father would never leave me on my own in this world, no matter what, because he knew no one loved me as much as he did. Linda and Mr Mia fought back their tears, and comforted me as best they could, staying with me until midnight.

I went upstairs to the bedroom to Sami. She was fast asleep. I gave her a hug and a kiss. I went back downstairs and sat in the dark all night. I thought about all the things he used to say to me, and I remembered once he said, 'When you are in England, if you see an old man in the street, I bet you'll think of me.' I thought of my last phone conversation with him, and the way he was talking to me as though he knew that he wasn't going to speak to me again. Soon, the realisation struck home that he had left me all alone.

I also thought about the time when I left Bangladesh, and seeing him waving me off at the coach station. Who would have known that that was the last time I was going to see my father? These random thoughts and memories swirled around in my mind all night.

The following day, I phoned my family in Bangladesh, and they tried to comfort me. The worst thing was not having been able to go to Bangladesh to visit my father before he died, because of everything that had happened with Nunu's family. I never managed to see my ill father for the last time, or even to mourn him properly after his death. But I knew I had to stay strong for Sami and my family in Bangladesh.

After I lost my father, I started to hate Nunu and his family even more; I became even more convinced that they were directly responsible for my father's illness and death. At one point, I even thought of going to their house and letting them know exactly what I thought of them all, and even lashing out physically if the opportunity arose, but then I stopped to think about Sami and my family. My father wouldn't have wanted me to do that, and I remembered my father saying, 'If you can control your mind when you are angry, then you won't have to suffer the consequences of your action later.'

A few weeks later, my brother Raj left Bangladesh for America. I know we never got on well as children but, as people grow older, they change. He has settled down now, so I'm happy for my brother. He never had an easy life, either, so he deserved a chance, and I was more than happy to help him. I'm happy when my family is happy; I love my family very much. One of my wishes is to see all my family members living together peacefully, tolerating each other in a loving environment, which was something missing from our childhood. It disappoints me that my two older brothers, who never got on with each other, are now both married and have their own children, but they still won't see eye to eye on many things. You would think they might have changed by now, but that's not always the case. I always try to help solve their problems and differences with love and understanding, but I suppose I'll have to accept that these two will never quite grow up.

At this stage, my father's death still hadn't sunk in, but I knew that I wasn't going to see him again. My feeling, though, is that he hasn't gone for eternity, he's with me constantly, looking out for me wherever he is. My mother often said to me that my personality was an exact replica of my father's, and I'm proud of that – I'm proud of being my father's daughter. It's a privilege and honour for me. I know I will never see him again, but he will always be with me.

I would say I'm someone who feels things very deeply, but I won't always show my emotions when the worst happens to me. This has a lot to do with my pride. Despite all the pain and sadness, I've never become depressed and, although physically I might become ill as my body tries to cope with the stress, mentally I would like to think I'm strong. I don't let depression touch me. I could never allow myself to fall into that dark hole. I just look for a way out of my problems and, eventually, I'll find the exit somehow.

Despite everything, I carried on with life, moving forward. I wasn't going to let anybody or anything defeat me. I think I just had to find the balance between my inner self and all the problems in my life. As a result of my father's death, within six months I had developed a completely different frame of mind. I noticed that I had changed; I approached everything as a personal challenge, and stopped caring what other people thought of me. I used to stop and think, but not any more. I also developed quite an attitude – if I didn't like a person for a good reason, they just didn't exist for me. And I never reacted to anything anyone said about me; I wouldn't validate their opinion with a reaction.

Some Asian women started to dislike me for adopting that attitude, but bitching about others isn't exclusive to any one culture

– it's everywhere, especially if you are a single Asian mother living by yourself. Gossip hurts me the most, and the way I dealt with it was by ignoring such people. That wasn't easy, but I had to look after my daughter and myself. From time to time, I went 'selectively blind' whenever I was around such people. Some Asian men tried to harass me as well, but they hadn't reckoned with my newfound confidence.

If I had listened to people's gossip and opinions, I would have stayed with Nunu and destroyed my life, along with my daughter's. I was quite clear about what I wanted and didn't bother about whether it would work in my case or not. My father said to me once, 'When people give you grief, if you don't let it affect you, then it will only affect those who are trying to put you down.' I tried my very best to put those words into action.

Over time, I started to consider bringing my daughter up differently from other children, to enable her to benefit from my principles and values. It's something that is very important to me. I want her growing up to be even more strong-minded than I am. With this in mind, I decided a few years later that I would encourage her to attend martial arts classes. I felt that it was very important to me to know that, when she is old enough, if she ever found herself in a difficult situation, she could at least stand up for herself. I wanted her to be the best martial artist around, and she will be one day.

Having received my qualifications from college, I was delighted and proud of myself, and started to look around for a job. After making some enquiries, one particular women's organisation suggested that, because of what I'd been through, perhaps I could help many other women going through similar problems. That organisation eventually took me on as a volunteer, and then they gave me access to various courses to become a fully qualified member of staff. From then on, I discovered that I could offer a great deal of help to women and children, particularly those from

Asian backgrounds who are victims of arranged marriages. I wanted to make a positive difference to those women's lives, and I was keen to do anything to help them. I knew that I could help because I could understand intimately what they were going through.

I had many aspirations, as well, and I still have. One day, I want to set up some sort of support organisation for women in Bangladesh, to help those who are going through what I went through. I know I would be able to make a difference.

As time went by, everyday life became more of a struggle for me. I was doing everything to the best of my ability, trying to make space for my daughter and myself within society as a whole. I was always trying to fit in with others, and I didn't know which way to turn at that point. Sometimes, I felt completely lost. But I always trusted my own instincts, no matter what, and that's the reason I haven't made any mistakes so far. I told myself, if I do make any mistakes, at least it's a heartfelt mistake. I guess I wanted to build a new identity for myself, so I moved on without knowing what was ahead of me.

My little Sami was now four years old, and it was time for her to start infant school. There she was, a tiny little thing, putting her little bag on her back, and trotting off to school. She even had a little boyfriend called Paul. Sometimes, after school, he used to cross the road holding his dad's finger and blowing kisses to my little Sami, who used to become very shy and start giggling. Perfectly normal behaviour for a four-year-old, I suppose!

I was very much aware of how careful I was in looking out for Sami – overprotective is probably more accurate – but I had to be; Nunu was still never very far away. He was always in the background, and I simply couldn't trust him or his family. Once he tried to make contact with Sami while she was at school and, when I found out, I could hardly contain my anger. How dare he try to get close to my daughter? Naturally, I became quite paranoid about Sami's safety, so I asked David, my solicitor, if he would help me by writing a letter to the school. He did write the letter, and that was a big help.

It was bad enough that I had to deal with Nunu, but, to add to my problems, I started to attract a lot of unwanted attention from some of the men from the local Asian community. This wasn't anything new, as this was normal practice, it seemed, for men whenever they got the chance, especially when they became aware of a single woman living by herself. Those idiots automatically thought that, because I was on my own, they could just ask me out and, if I said no, then they had the right to harass me. Any single Asian woman living on her own has probably experienced this at some point, and everyone knows just how pathetic and stupid a man has to be to behave in this way.

Some of these idiots would knock on my door in the middle of the night, or call me names whenever I did my shopping. They'd gossip about why I was divorcing Nunu, and look at me really strangely when I passed them in the street. It all became very difficult to cope with. Even some Asian women started to treat me differently, and some of them went as far as saying that I should get married for the sake of my daughter, otherwise I would give the community a bad name.

There was also talk about me wearing Western clothes. I found this hard to accept, as I was hardly wearing mini-skirts and crop tops! If I chose to wear Western clothes, I'd always choose some trousers and a long top or something similar, because there is no way I would ever have worn anything that showed my body. I strongly believed that, if I did wear something glamorous and revealing, that should only be for the man I love.

I think the reason behind this criticism is the fact that people are often confused over what is modern and what is Western; there is a huge difference between the two. For example, I could never consider myself 'Western', as that would be ridiculous. But, yes, I'm a modern woman who has deep-seated Bangladeshi cultural values. End of story.

I'm not saying that we can't learn from the West, as there's clearly so much we can learn from each other, but we often let our egos get in the way. And that's true when you look beyond the general population at some of our world leaders. This is the twenty-first century and they still have to bomb each other to get their point across.

Another issue I was faced with, which many Asian women would undoubtedly agree with me on, was the fact that part of our Asian society still thrives on double standards. What right did those Asian men have to look down on me? Their reason was because I was getting divorced, and that I had become a single woman living by myself. I also chose not to wear the *hijab*, and I was brave enough to hold my head up high, and face up to life without a man controlling me. It must also have annoyed them that I had a few male friends from college.

There were many men I came across who held this narrow view of the world and caused me a great number of problems. They needed to open their eyes, and widen their horizons. I wondered why men weren't treated in the same way. Why did Asian men get away with everything?

I would like to say to those Asian men who continue to treat Asian women in this way, 'Ask your parents to teach you how to respect women, because we Asian women deserve more respect. Just think how you would feel if one of my brothers treated your mother or sister with the same contempt right in front of you. It's as simple as that!

'If you aren't a real man – if you're someone who picks on single women – don't come anywhere near me. Live your own life and let me live mine. And don't be fooled by my innocent looks, either!

Looks can be deceptive, so do not push me too far, as you'll never win. I don't have money, muscle or any political influence – but I've got a brain, and I use it!'

Well, I can't change the way I am now or what I believe and, as it hasn't worked against me so far, why should I bother?

I was really fed up with being a victim again and again. I didn't want to be a victim any more, I wanted to be loved and respected. All I wanted was a little space for my daughter and myself in society, and I wanted to give my daughter the best of everything, even things that I never had as a child.

I must admit I had some great friends. One particular friend – Luke, an Italian Muslim, who was very good-looking – I met while I was at Newcastle College. We were good friends, and he cared about me a lot, especially Sami. After a while, we both started to regard each other as a little bit more than just friends. What I really liked about him was that he valued me as a person, and accepted me for what I was. Whenever we were together, I would just cuddle up to him on the sofa for hours. He never put any pressure on me to make the relationship more intimate, because he knew very well what I had just gone through. He also knew that I would never feel comfortable in an intimate relationship without being in love or being married. That was really important to me.

Spending time with Luke giving me endless cuddles meant so much to me. We shared a great deal of understanding. Sometimes, I used to cuddle up to him and say to him that I just wanted to go to sleep on his chest, and that he shouldn't wake me up until the morning. He used to hold me tight with a smile and say, 'Go to sleep.'

I used to fall asleep like a baby. I was so tired emotionally, and I was tired of my struggle to survive and provide a good life for my daughter. So it was a wonderful way for me to forget about everything. For some reason, we couldn't give our relationship a name; maybe that was for the best, as we certainly weren't in love with each other.

Deep down, I knew what I wanted – to meet somebody, fall in love, get married and live happily ever after. And it had to be with somebody who would love me and Sami unconditionally; somebody who understood how vulnerable I was emotionally; somebody who understood me completely; somebody who would love me the way I need to be loved; only then would we be able to enjoy each other in a complete and fulfilling way.

After a while, Luke and I decided that, because we didn't love each other as a couple, we should just remain friends, and we continued in that vein for a few years. Eventually, he went back to Italy and got married there. I wish him well in life. Thanks, Luke, for filling my empty life with some love and affection, and for your endless cuddles. I'm sorry I couldn't love you the way you wanted me to.

10 UNCHAIN MY HEART

Finally on 20 April 1994, I received really good news – I got my divorce papers! God, I was so happy that I decided to throw a big party at my house and invited all my friends, and they also organised a night out in Manchester. We decided to go to an Indian dinner and dance club and I really enjoyed myself. It's amazing, really, that that was my very first night out in my entire life. I'll never forget that night; I even took my Sami with me because it was a special family night out as far as I was concerned.

So, at last, I was free from Nunu and all the problems that surrounded him. I felt as though I had just won my longest, hardest battle. I cried a lot that night, thinking to myself that, if my father had still been alive, he would have been really happy for me.

After I divorced Nunu, I seriously don't know what came over me – I stopped being concerned about anybody or anything else. I did whatever I felt like doing. I started to despise Asian people and I adopted a very aggressive attitude towards them, especially those who looked down on me for being a single mother.

I also started to hate living in the West End of Newcastle. I wanted to move out and, at one point, I wanted to go back to Bangladesh as well, to see my father's grave and be close to him, and to see all my family again. And none of my family had seen Sami yet, so that would have been nice. But how could I go? Going there might have meant losing my little Sami, and there was no way I would take that risk. She is more precious to me than anything, and I will protect her until my last breath.

At times like that I needed some guidance and advice, something I've only ever had from my father. Generally, I've had to pick up all the pieces by myself; I've had no one else to fall back on.

Some of my relatives from Bangladesh said at that time that I should go back to Bangladesh, where they would find me another nice man to marry! I thought, 'Not another one! One arranged marriage is enough for me!' I told my mother to put a stop to that nonsense, as I wasn't living up to anybody else's expectations any longer.

That added bit of pressure put me off the idea of ever going back to Bangladesh. I strongly believed that, if I did return, they would force me to get married again, and there was no way I was going to let anybody destroy my life again. I'd got to the point that, if anyone even mentioned the word 'marriage' to me, I'd become so frightened that I used to have terrifying nightmares about arranged marriages.

For the first time, I became quite resentful towards my own family and relatives, and it was difficult for me not to blame them for getting me married off in the first place. I know, obviously, that they weren't all to blame, and I seriously don't know what possessed me, but I wrote a very hurtful letter to my mother and brother, saying that they had destroyed my life. I also reminded them that, despite that, I had helped them through their difficulties. That was really the most upsetting thing I could ever have said to them, because, in my culture, if you do something to help your family, especially when they are in need, you should never bring it up later to show off or make them feel guilty. I know it would have hurt them badly. I even stopped writing to them for a while, thinking that, if my father had still been there for me, everything would have been all right.

Within a few weeks, I moved out of our first home. I just wanted a new start for my baby and me. Nobody else mattered to me any more. After everything that I had had to go through, I felt the constant need to be strong and determined, and the result was that I became selfish and heartless. We moved to another part of Newcastle called Fowdon, but I was so angry with my family that I never even told them where we'd gone. That was my way of punishing them for not understanding my needs or my feelings, and it made me feel good to lash out at them like that. In fact, I only gave my address to very few close friends, so my family couldn't find out where I was unless I wanted them to. I never considered for a moment that they might be worried about me.

By this time, I had developed such a loathing for Asian men that I stopped wearing Asian clothes altogether. I used to wear a lot of Western clothes – jeans and tops – which I felt extremely uncomfortable in, but I still wore them to fit in with other English people. One way of explaining this could be that I was trying to wipe out all my links to the negative side of Asian culture.

I found a job in a women's group, where I had been working as a support worker in their centre on a voluntary basis hoping it would lead to a paid position. It was only a part-time job, because my Sami was still very young. I didn't like the idea of leaving her with a childminder and going to work from nine to five.

One day, a friend of mine invited me to her birthday party, which took place in a local nightclub. I had never been to a nightclub before, so I told her that I felt uncomfortable coming along. She persuaded me to go, though, so I went, and asked a very close friend to look after Sami for the night. The nightclub turned out to be aboard a boat on the Tyne, called the Tuxedo Royal. It was very impressive, and soon I met up with all my friends, some of whom were drinking alcohol. One of them offered me to drink, saying that, if I drank it up, all my pain would disappear. Well, I didn't want to touch it, as I'd never drunk alcohol before. But, as the night wore on, I felt I wanted to fit in with the others, and thought to myself, 'What harm can one drink do?' So I had a glass of wine. I immediately felt sick and threw up in the toilet. 'How can people drink alcohol?' I wondered.

From that day on, I started to go out once a week with my friends. Although I never wanted to drink alcohol again, I couldn't stop thinking about what my friend had said – if I had a drink, then I'd forget all my problems. But my biggest problem was that I couldn't stand the smell of alcohol, no matter what type it was!

One night, I ended up making a fool of myself. I went to a nightclub with my friends, having decided that, no matter what happened, I'd drink that evening until I got drunk. Somehow, I managed to drink a few glasses of Malibu, but the only way I could manage it was to hold the glass in one hand and my nose in the other! That way, I couldn't smell the alcohol. My friends couldn't stop laughing.

After a while, I must have become extremely drunk. I can't remember exactly what happened, but I started to become completely uncontrollable, laughing happily one minute, and the next I'd be in tears. Then I sat down in the middle of the table and thought to myself, 'I know that I've drunk a lot of Malibu tonight, but all my pain is still here in my heart.' It hurt me physically, to the extent that I could feel nothing but pain.

Since that day, I have never touched another drop of alcohol, and I never will. I realised that drinking alcohol would never make me pain free; for that, I needed love and emotional security.

I dated a few Asian men on different occasions but, unfortunately, none of those relationships worked for me; there was no getting away from the fact that I was a single mother, and

I was apparently too modern for an Asian woman. None of them could offer me the sort of special love and affection that I was looking for. Or maybe I was just too intelligent for them! Most importantly, none of them understood me at all.

This period of abandoning my roots and thinking only of myself went on for around seven months. Eventually, the reality of my situation hit me squarely in the face. Sami had a touch of 'flu one day, on the day that I usually went out. Deep down, I didn't really want to go out that night because of Sami's illness, but my friend who regularly looked after Sami, Rubina, eventually persuaded me to go out. I knew that Sami was in very good hands, because Rubina used to work for a children's organisation, and she'd been very good to Sami and me.

So I got ready to go out, and at about 9.00pm my friend picked me up from my house. I gave Sami a kiss and cuddle before I left, but my poor little baby didn't want me to go. I told her that I'd come back soon, so she accepted that.

We arrived at a club called Julie. My friend kept on reassuring me that Sami would be all right, so I shouldn't worry as she only had a bit of 'flu. When she said that, I lost my temper with her and said to her, 'What sort of person are you? How can you say that? I should be at home with my baby!' I immediately ran outside and got in a taxi to come straight home. Rubina was surprised to see me home so early, but she left soon afterwards, saying that Sami was feeling a lot better and she had gone to sleep.

I went up to Sami and cuddled up to her. I then asked myself some very serious questions – what the hell had I been doing for the last seven months? What had I been doing to myself? Why had I been going to clubs and trying to drink alcohol? It just wasn't me! That wasn't the real me at all! Why was I trying to be somebody I wasn't? How could I be so cruel to my own family in Bangladesh and not write to them for seven months? Good God, they must have been devastated not knowing where I was. How could I put my family through something like that? How could I have so much loathing for all Asian people when only a few individuals had been responsible for what had happened to me? How could I forget my values?

I cried all night. There and then, I was full of remorse and thanked God for giving me the sense to make amends. That night, I returned to my real self. I rang my mother that night and cried like a child, asking her to forgive me for being so stubborn. She was relieved to hear from me, because they were in the process of writing to the British authorities to find out if I was all right and to track me and Sami down. I also felt very guilty and ashamed of myself for putting them through such a nightmare.

I promised my family that I would never do anything like that again. That made me feel better and, since that day, I've never been clubbing nor touched any alcohol again. I was very happy to have my old self back after that, and felt proud that I'd managed to turn things around on my own. Whenever I go out now, I stick to water and, if anyone has a problem with that, then tough! I don't have any problem with someone sitting next to me and drinking all day long, it doesn't bother me, as long as others accept the fact that I'm sitting next to them only drinking water. I'd much rather be intoxicated with love, if you ask me!

I started to concentrate on Sami's and my future, and from then on I kept in close touch with my family. Sami was doing very well in school, but I decided to start a new life away from Newcastle. That way, Nunu would find it much more difficult to darken our door again. Sooner or later, he would find out where I lived locally, and then he would start harassing me again. I simply couldn't breathe the same air as Nunu any longer.

I talked to my housing manager and requested a housing transfer to London. My main reasons for choosing the capital were because

My brother Joynal with my niece outside the house I grew up in.

Above: My father's grave, which I still haven't visited yet.

Right: My father, a legend to me. My life hasn't been the same since he passed away.

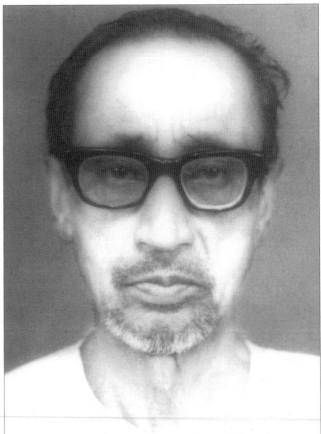

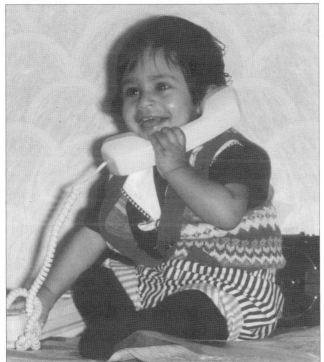

Above: My angel, with a couple of friends!

Left: My little Sami as a baby talking to my father for the first time.

In the traditional Asian bridal dress that I wore when I married Charlie.

How *The Mirror* reported my marriage.

Above: A scene from the play where I visit Charlie in prison.

Right: The poster for the play that was written about my life.

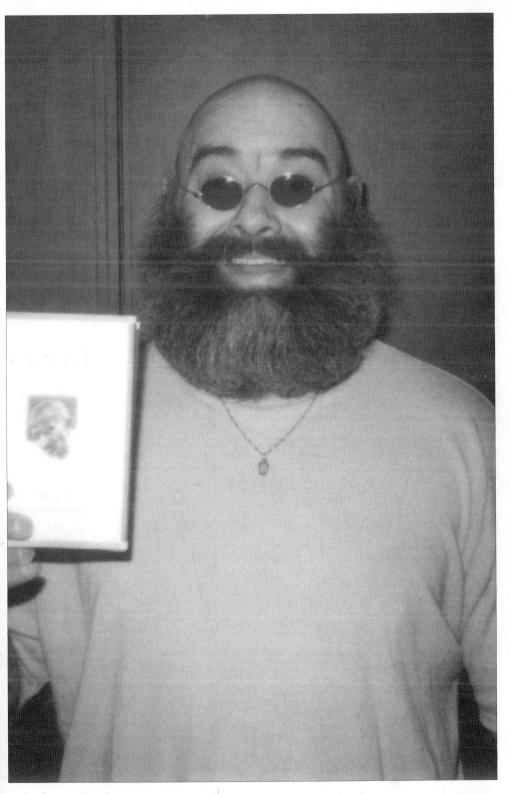

After we married Charlie converted to Islam and took my father's name to be called Ali Charles Ahmed. He is pictured here holding a copy of Gandhi's autobiography.

Top: Sami is training to be strong like her mum! Here she is with her Karate instructor.

Above: With friends on a night out. On the right is Bhabna and in the middle is Hansa.

I wanted to get as far away as possible from Nunu, I wanted to get a good job and I also wanted to study at an Indian classical dance academy, as that yearning I had as a child to learn Indian classical dance had never really gone away.

One day, as usual, when I went to pick up Sami from school, one of her teachers said to me that a man had appeared saying that he was Sami's father and he wanted to see her. I couldn't believe what I was hearing. I was so frightened that I didn't take Sami to school for a week. We stayed in our house, and, when we eventually did venture out, I was constantly looking over my shoulder for fear of Nunu suddenly snatching Sami away from me. I couldn't cope with this indefinitely, so I contacted my housing manager again and asked her to rush through our move. Within a week, she came to see me with the news that she had found a property ... but it wasn't in London.

I didn't have long to decide whether we wanted to take her up on the offer of a house in what could be our new home town – Luton in Bedfordshire. It was the nearest place to London she could find. To be honest, there wasn't really a choice to make, considering the fact that Nunu had been attempting to make contact with Sami, so I accepted the offer to move to Luton. A friend of mine helped me with the move and, apart from telling two very close friends, I decided to keep our whereabouts absolutely secret.

As we headed towards the motorway leaving Newcastle behind us, I thought to myself that, as long as I live, I'll never come back to Newcastle again. For some strange reason, I felt sorry for the lost soul I used to be in Newcastle. I wiped my tears and looked straight ahead, like a warrior ready for any battle that might come her way. I just smiled as I enjoyed the taste of victory.

Our move to Luton was in 1996. To begin with, I changed Sami's and my name, as I didn't want to give Nunu the opportunity of finding out where we lived. I used to be known as Fatema Rehman, but I changed my name to Saira Ahmed; Ahmed is actually my father's surname. As for Sami, I changed Sami Rehman to Sami Ahmed. I felt very safe in Luton; nobody knew me there, so I never had to look over my shoulder every time I went out. I had long ago decided that I would never compromise, except when it came to my loved ones. Sami had to be protected, so a compromise was the best route forward at the time.

My house is in the middle of the Asian community, which was a concern for me given my single-parent status. Then again, I was quite good at keeping myself to myself and, as long as I did that, I should be all right. When Sami started her new school – Denbigh Infants – it gave me some time to look for a job and mix with some nice people.

One day, I met a wonderful Asian lady called Nasira Mahmud. She was working in a women's organisation at that time, where they support the victims of domestic violence, provide all sorts of information services and run courses for women. They also work very closely with the local community-based organisations, such as the police, Women's Aid, Home Start, some Asian women's groups and so on.

Nasira and I become friends after a while, and soon I came to regard her as my older sister. A few weeks later, she took me to her workplace – the Luton All Women's Centre – and showed me round. I was looking for a full-time job, but they didn't have any vacancies, although they were prepared to take me on as a volunteer and give me the necessary training, which was exactly what I needed. Then, as soon as a paid position came along, I would be in a much stronger position to apply for a job there.

That was good enough for me. I started to work there four days a week. It was a good start, and I loved working there. My colleagues were very supportive, particularly Karen Guest, Minoo Beach and the Chairperson, Jabeen Jaffry, from the management team. I'll always be grateful to them.

While all this was going on, I started to make enquiries about Indian classical dance as well. I'd always been madly in love with the form of classical dance called Kathak, which means 'telling stories'. The dance itself requires a lot of hand movements and footwork, and incorporates elaborate physical gestures. The effect is as though you're watching poetry with the most beautiful instrumental accompaniment. Whenever I see someone dancing Kathak, it's as though I'm watching an angel dancing on a cloud.

After phoning a few places, I found a dance company in Luton called Kadam Dance Showcase. I joined them and then used to go every weekend, taking my Sami with me; she used to love going there to watch her mum dancing. I made some nice friends as well, although I was still wary of new people because I had been deceived and abused so many times.

At around this time, I also became involved with an Asian cultural dance group in London, which I really enjoyed. It make me feel so good about things whenever we got the chance to perform in a theatre. It was as though an unknown power took me over and I could lose myself only to love and happiness. Having had this ambition since childhood, dancing helps me enormously; it frees me from my pain for a short while. I would recommend classical dance to anyone in need of a similar release from stress and suffering – believe me, it's extremely therapeutic.

Roughly six months went by. By then, I had developed enormously at my work because of all the training. My colleagues were very impressed with me, so the management team gave me more responsibility. I was now dealing with young Asian women who were victims of forced/arranged marriages; I helped victims of domestic violence and I was sorting out housing issues. So I had an important and varied job to do, and I enjoyed it enormously. I still feel so grateful to Karen and Minoo, who had faith in me, and gave me the opportunity I needed.

The women's centre was mainly a referral organisation, and most of the time we had to deal with other organisations as well, such as Women's Aid, housing associations, social services, the police and many more. As time went by, I became too attached to my work. I felt that, by helping all the women who needed my assistance, I was making a positive difference to their lives, and I felt that I could understand and relate to them at a very deep level because of what I'd been through myself.

One year later, I was well established at the women's centre, and qualified for a paid position there – I was the training co-ordinator for the volunteers we were recruiting at the centre. It was only a starting point, but it meant a lot to me. I was very happy, and felt that I could contribute something important to the centre.

Although I now had a paid role there, I still worked a lot of my time as a volunteer. My plan was to gain more experience, so, one day, I would be able to run my own support network for women and children.

At this point, one of my main roles at the centre was to deal with Asian women of all age groups. At that time, I was the only Asian person working there who was capable of speaking Bengali, Hindi and Urdu as well as English, so the elder Asian ladies found that very helpful. As far as the younger Asian women were concerned, most of them used to come to us with arranged/forced marriage problems. I helped as much as I could, despite the fact that we weren't allowed to give advice to them. Sometimes, I would refer them to the relevant authorities, or I just listened to them.

One day, I really got myself into trouble. In my local area, a lot of Asian women knew that I was working at the women's centre, so I often used to get approached by them for help. I would just give them my office number, so they could come and see me there.

As often happened, a young Asian girl approached me for help while I was out and about. She was in love with somebody and her parents wanted to send her to Pakistan to get married to somebody else. The marriage was already arranged. So I said to her that, as it was a weekend, I wouldn't be able to help her at all until the following Monday. I also gave her the emergency number for the Luton Women's Aid. With that, she walked off.

Later on that day, I got home to find that young lady standing on my doorstep with a suitcase. Obviously, she had known exactly where I lived. She was very upset and started to say that she didn't want to go to a women's refuge, so would I be kind enough to let her stay at my house for a couple days, until her boyfriend found a place?

I felt very sorry for her, and I could see that she was very distressed. I let her stay that day, wondering whether I had done the right thing. That night, I rang one of my colleagues and talked to her about the situation. She didn't think that it had been terribly sensible letting her stay in my house, as her family could become very aggressive towards me. She certainly had a point.

But it was too late now, because I was already involved. The next day, I went to do some shopping at my local store with Sami. I left the young lady at my house, as I didn't think taking her out was a wise idea under the circumstances. I was just at the end of my road when three cars pulled up right front of me. Each one was full of Asian men. I did not have a clue what was going on. Before I knew it, they all got out of their cars and started to shout at me, accusing me of influencing their sister to leave the house. By then, the penny had well and truly dropped.

One of them started saying, 'You bitches at the women's centre … that's all you do! Influence our young girls …'

I told him that I got paid for that! They then demanded to know where I had hidden their sister. There was no way I was going to tell them where she was, because I knew what she would face after that – they would have beaten her up then shoved her on the next plane to Pakistan!

At that point, one of them started to get a bit aggressive and said to his friend, 'Give her a slap, then she'll tell us where our sister is.'

'Don't even think about it!' I snapped. 'You'll regret it … especially while I've got my little baby with me.'

By then, a black man had stopped his car and approached us, saying, 'Hey, guys, stop it … it's embarrassing to see you picking on her; she's one of your own people!'

After that, they left. I couldn't believe that they'd thrown all that crap at me like that on the street! I had Sami with me as well, but they couldn't have cared less. It was obvious to me that their parents had forgotten to teach them to respect women and children.

Apparently, those bullies had all been her brothers and cousins. I was glad I didn't have ten cousins and brothers in Luton who cared about me as much as that! I got back to the house and described what had happened to the young lady, telling her that I couldn't get any more involved than I was. I made it clear that she'd have to go to Women's Aid for help, and I personally organised somebody from that organisation to pick her up. She left soon afterwards, but I still had her brothers knocking on my door all night. In the end, I couldn't take any more and called the police, but the rest of the weekend was spent dealing with the repercussions. I promised myself then that, no matter who turned up on my doorstep, I'd never allow anyone else to put me in that position again. I'd learned my lesson!

The following Monday, when I got to work, my boss told me off for helping the woman in that way. And the problem didn't end there; that woman's family kept on harassing me for ages after that. They were one sick family! Every now and then, they used to send different men to come and knock on my door, but I never answered the door or talked to them. Sometimes, they'd even come knocking at 1.00am or 2.00am, and shout insults through the letterbox! Again, all I could do was call the police and report the incidents. I was never frightened of those idiots – they were just cowards picking on a single woman – my only concern was Sami.

Sami is my main priority, so I didn't want idiots like that upsetting her. At that point in my life, I was too confident to let something like that bother me, so most of the time I ignored them if I could. I had become someone who didn't take any nonsense from anybody. After a while, they stopped harassing me, but that left me with a big problem. Lots of people knew that I was a single woman living by myself, and that I worked for an organisation that supported women who were escaping from forced/arranged marriages, or who were the victims of domestic violence. My overriding concern was that I didn't want anybody to find out that I had moved from Newcastle, and risk Nunu being able to trace me.

There were many Asian people who respected me for having helped the local Asian community, and also for having coped with my own difficult circumstances. But there was also a significant group of idiots who tried regularly to make my life hell, some of whom regarded me as a sort of curse on their society and values. Some parents even feel threatened by me, and won't allow their daughters, wives or sisters to mix with me, in case they follow my example or try to emulate me! The simple truth is, I don't have any intention of influencing anyone – I just do what's best for my daughter and me. Maybe if they tried to do the same, then their daughters wouldn't feel the need to run away. Sadly, I do feel a little let down by a small sector of my own community, and my own family, as my thoughts and feelings were never listened to unless they corresponded to what everyone else saw as the right way of doing things.

This is one of the main problems some Asian families have, if not most families. They have not managed to achieve a relationship with their children which is based on openness and understanding. Perhaps I can explain this better using my own circumstances as an example: I've got what I believe is a very good relationship with my daughter. We are like friends. And I am sure that, if you asked me in another five, ten or even twenty years what my relationship with my daughter is like, I can assure you that it will be as solid as ever. We talk about everything. We are so open and trusting with each other that I deeply believe that, when she is old enough and she starts to date men, I will be the first one she tells, rather than hearing it from the police because she's run away from home. I have brought her up to be like that, and I'm proud of the way I've managed to do that.

Don't misunderstand me, though – I have also taught her important Bangladeshi cultural values, and I've tried to offer her a good balance of modern influences as well. So my daughter's got it all; the rest I'll leave to God, as there's only so much I can do!

My point is that I think it's very important to have an open, respectful relationship with your children. When they are older, they will then feel more inclined to discuss things and ask for advice before making difficult decisions. Cultural and religious values are part and parcel of this process, and shouldn't be forgotten either. I firmly believe that a good balance of all these things helps us to be the best parents we can be.

As if I didn't have enough to occupy my time by this point, some of my close friends sometimes used to try to fix me up with Asian men in the area. I must admit, I went along with it for a bit, but that was one big mistake. Asian men in Luton have massive attitude problems. As far as my experience with men goes, most of them don't understand the word 'respect'. I know a lot of Asian women would probably agree with me on this. It took me a long time before I realised why that was and, in my case, the reason was simple – I was a single woman living on my own. They automatically thought that, if there is single, modern-thinking Asian woman living on her own, she must be really desperate, or a push-over, so therefore she can just be used and treated without much consideration.

Whenever I turned up on a date or got to know one of these men, I was usually faced with this sort of attitude. One had a wife at home but forgot to tell me! Once, I met a really nice man but we didn't get on very well, so I didn't want to see him any more. But he wouldn't take 'no' for an answer, so he used to knock on my door after midnight every night. Eventually, I had to call the police. After that, just to make things even more upsetting for me, he went and told all his male friends to come and knock on my door after midnight as well. He used to phone me saying that he wouldn't let me live a normal life because I wouldn't go out with him. He made my life very difficult for a while and, whenever I went out, his idiot friends always picked on me. With all my experience of dealing with Nunu and his problems, I could have recommended a few good mental hospitals to this guy – a short weekend break there would probably have done him the power of good!

Seriously, life started to become unbearable for me; every night, after sending Sami to bed, I used to sit and wonder when some stupid idiot was going to knock on my door. The stress surrounding something like that isn't easy to deal with, and I pray that they appreciate one day just how much trauma they put me through. I wouldn't wish anyone else to suffer as I did, but if their sister or mother experienced the same thing, perhaps only then they'd appreciate just how malicious and hurtful their behaviour was.

Every night, I used to double-check the locks on my doors and windows, then, before I went to sleep, I used to put a pot of chilli powder next to my bed. Then, if someone broke into my house, all I needed was a handful of this burning powder. Believe me, if he got a load of chilli powder in his eyes, he would soon forget why he broke into my house! And just to be clear about this, I didn't just buy chilli powder as a weapon – I used it every day in my cooking, so I always had a plentiful supply for both purposes!

I liked another Pakistani man, but he only wanted to go out with me when it was dark! He never wanted to see me during the daytime, because he was a 'well-respected' person within the Asian community, and he didn't want people to find out that he was dating a 'single' Asian woman. I showed him the door and gave him a bit of free advice, too – instead of me serving him, he should stick to serving the community!

There was another strange man, whose hobby was picking strawberries at the weekend. Somehow, I couldn't imagine myself picking strawberries all the time. I don't like strawberries, anyway; they're not sweet enough for me!

After all these failed dates, I completely steered clear of Asian men in Luton, because I'd learned my lesson the hard way. And I knew very well where these attitudes came from. Often, their parents worked very hard to provide the best for their children, so most of these idiots got spoiled from an early age. They had hardly ever experienced any hardship living in England, although, occasionally, they might be taken to Bangladesh, Pakistan or India for a few weeks' holiday. That is their only opportunity to see how poor people struggle in those countries. So most of them live in England in luxury, forgetting what humanity is. They forget that they are Asian, too, and that they are treating another Asian – a woman – like an object to be used or insulted. I swear to God, if any of them had been my son, I would have taken him to Bangladesh and left him there until he became a proper human being! My father was right when he used to say that, just because you look like a human being, it doesn't mean you are one! You must have the qualities of a human being to be one.

Of course, I'm not saying all people in Bangladesh are angels; there are good and bad all over the world. We are not one of the richest countries in the world, either, but we are rich in our values, principles and the wonderful culture. For example, if you go to a poor person's house as a guest, he or she would offer you their last bit of food to eat, just because you are their guest. They wouldn't think about whether they might remain hungry or not. If any of my brothers had behaved like that towards women, knowing my mother, she would have laid into them with both fists!

There were, though, a few nice Asian people I'd met in Luton, who accepted me for what I was. They didn't love me, but they didn't hate me, either, and that's exactly how it should be.

Some of these people even call me weird. Maybe I am weird! My favourite cartoon character is Tweety pie (the little yellow bird) from Sylvester and Tweety pie. I love it so much because Tweety always escapes death by the evil cat Sylvester. You can learn a lot from that little bird. I'm also a big fan of the American rapper Eminem. I think he comes up with some of the best lyrics. So, maybe I am a weird person!

I became much more involved at work with lots of different projects. At that stage, most of my time was spent at the women's centre on a voluntary basis. But I still undertook my paid role there as a training co-ordinator. I was funded by the women's centre itself and, although there wasn't much of a salary, I was happy. I knew very well that, as soon as a full-time position came along, I would stand a good chance of being offered it, so I was more than happy to wait.

The management team seemed very impressed with all I was doing. By that time, I had been at the women's centre for two years, and I had taken on an increasing number of responsibilities there. I become one of the reporting officers on behalf of the centre for racial harassment, and I had started my own 'recycling' project, which enabled some of my neediest clients to get hold of second-hand clothing, small items of furniture, toys for children, dry food, cutlery and so on. That was my little way of trying to help those who struggled to make ends meet.

I also become involved with other community groups and did a lot of voluntary work whenever I had the time. One particular organisation I really enjoyed working with was a Bangladeshi women's group based in Luton. That's where I met one of my closest friends, Caroline Islam, whom I regard as a sister. She is from Bangladesh as well, has two children, and has experienced some of life's hardships, too. I wish her all the happiness in the world. We have always been there for each other, and I really value her professional support and the subsequent friendship that grew over time. I love Caroline like a sister, and deeply appreciate all the love she has shown Sami and me.

With all my good friends, my work, Sami to look after and my dancing to pursue, I had little time for much socialising, but, when one of my friends invited me to her birthday celebration, I thought it would make a really nice change. We booked a table in an Indian dinner-dance restaurant called Piano, in London, and there were about ten of us sitting together, enjoying the live Indian music played by a band from India.

After a few minutes, I noticed that one of the male singers kept looking at me while he was performing. I just smiled and left it at that, but, after I'd watched him and talked to him for most of the evening, we both realised that we liked each other a lot. Later on that night, I left my phone number for him to call me.

He called me the next day, and asked me to come back to the club again as he wanted to see me. The next night, I went to the club with a friend of mine and, as soon as he saw me, his whole face lit up. He had the most amazing smile, and his eyes easily gave away how much he liked me. My friend and I were there until 2.30am, and all the while we just couldn't take our eyes off each other, especially when he was singing all the romantic songs.

Later on that week, we met up properly in Wembley, where he lived. The very first thing he did was to give me a cuddle, and he said, 'Saira, don't make me fall in love with you, as I'm only in England for three months. Then I have to go back to India.'

I felt as though my heart had stopped for a moment. He explained that he was touring with his band and, even if he had wanted to stay in England, it wouldn't be possible due to his family back home, as they were against the idea. They would never have accepted me, anyway, because I'm a Muslim and Jay was Hindu. On top of all that, I already had a child, and I was a divorcée. If Jay went against his parents' wishes then, obviously, they would end up disowning him, but none of this could have stopped us feeling the way we did about each other.

Sometimes, Jay used to say to me, 'Saira, in three months I'll give you a whole lifetime of love, so you won't miss me when I'm gone!' We used to meet up in a park in Wembley, where we'd talk and cuddle up to each other all day. Sometimes, he used to sit me down on his lap and sing to me. Then, in the evening, he had to go to the club to perform, and I went back to Luton. But he used to phone me every night after finishing his show, and the very first question he used to ask was, 'Sweetheart, have you eaten yet?' He knew that I liked to wait until he'd finished his show, then I would eat at the same time as him, as I felt guilty eating while he was working until very late at night. Sometimes, he used to tell me off for doing that!

Once a week, he used to come to Luton to see me and Sami, whom he really loved. We tried our best not to think about the fact that the three months would come to an end soon, when he would have to leave for good. But, eventually, the day inevitably got closer, until I knew that at the end of the week, on Friday, Jay would be flying back to India.

For some reason, Jay came to see me on Monday, and was behaving very strangely that day. He was extremely loving towards me, as though there was no tomorrow, telling me to look after Sami and myself properly after he had gone. He even sat me down on his lap and fed me some food with his own hand. Later on, at about 7.00pm, he left.

That night, I waited all night but Jay never rang. I found that strange, as he had never forgotten to phone me at night, no matter how late it was. I was worried, so I phoned the club owner at about 2.30am to ask if Jay was all right. The owner said that the band had left two hours earlier for the airport, to catch the flight to India. I dropped the receiver and sank to the floor. Slowly, I realised why Jay had never told me the actual departure date; he knew that I wouldn't be able to let him go. And I now understood why he had been behaving as if there was no tomorrow – there *was* no tomorrow!

I felt very lonely, as I was, once again, on my own. I had to forget about Jay as if it had all been a beautiful dream; greedy as I was for love, I had to move on and be strong again.

Suddenly, after all these years in England, I was really missing my family in Bangladesh. Not a day went by when I didn't think about them, and not a day goes by when I don't dream of going to Bangladesh. Even at night when I go to sleep, I have strange dreams about my family and friends in Bangladesh, as though I'm there with my mother or my little brother in our house, or I can see myself taking Sami to show her which school I went to. Often, I have the same dream in which I go back to Bangladesh and, as soon as I walk into our house, I go from room to room looking for my father, calling out for him at the same time. But I can't seem to find him anywhere. After that, I wake up in the middle of the night feeling deeply upset and sweating from head to toe. Eventually, I'll fall asleep again, and then I wake up in the morning and I start cursing my ex-husband and his family!

11 CHARLIE

You don't need to see God to worship him ... and I didn't need to know anything about this stranger to fall in love. You could fall in love with someone on the other side of the earth, or you may never even have met him, yet your heart still beats for them. Over time, gradually, that person becomes so close to you that they almost become part of you. It can happen ... and that is precisely what happened to me. This didn't happen in my case because of a deep-seated fascination or an infatuation; it was like a sort of magnetism that simply pulled us together. It's my belief that love and worship can sometimes be experienced in very similar ways.

Emotionally, I had become tired of everything. I almost started to believe that there wasn't anyone for me. At times, I used to feel as though God himself had forgotten to provide my perfect partner for me. My daily routine consisted of getting up in the morning, taking Sami to school, then going to the office, doing my work and coming home. After that, I usually did some dance practice; I still do. At 3.15 in the afternoon I used to pick up my little Sami from school. Then, once a week, I used to go to London to do my dance shows, and to socialise with friends. I never mixed with people in Luton after getting used to the area and some of the people. So that was basically my day-to-day life.

Finally, at about 8.30pm, once my Sami had gone to bed, I used to turn the light off in the living room and lie in the dark. That was often the time I used to feel I could almost touch happiness, but it still seemed just out of reach. That was the only time emotionally I felt truly alone.

Occasionally, the mental pain I felt could almost be sensed physically in my heart. But I always try to believe that nothing is out of your reach; you only have to keep reaching up to it and, when you do feel your fingers tighten around it, never let it go.

The only time I used to forget about everything was when I performed my classical dancing on stage. Even now, whenever I practise my dancing at home, I can easily forget about everything around me.

My mother often used to ring me from Bangladesh and tell me that I should go back there to find the man of my dreams. Even though she meant well, my only thought was, 'Never again!' Deep down, I felt that I could never trust any Asian man again after what I'd been through. I could be wrong, but that's how I felt.

At the same time, I felt sorry for my mother, because obviously she wanted to do something to make Sami and me happy. On the other hand, I sometimes felt quite ·sad, because most of Sami's friends had fathers, but Sami didn't. I would rather have no father for Sami than have that terrible man, though, and under no circumstances would he be allowed to come anywhere near my Sami. I became happier when Sami was old enough to understand why I had left Nunu, and that our family life was different from her friends' for good reason.

Life, however, has a strange and wonderful way of surprising you. It moves on and nothing can stop it. One day, something extraordinary happened.

It was the weekend and, in the morning, Sami was sitting in front of the television watching a *Tom and Jerry* cartoon. I realised that there wasn't any milk for breakfast, so I went to our local shop, grabbed some milk and picked up a local newspaper, the *Luton News*, as well. I don't normally read the newspaper, but every now and then I like to have a look at what's going on locally. I came home, made the breakfast and read through the paper as I was eating.

After I'd read a few pages, I saw an article about a prison inmate called Charles Bronson, accompanied by a little photo of him. I knew the name, but this clearly wasn't the actor! I remember reading the article, which mentioned why he'd gone to prison, but I can't remember why there was an article about him that particular day. I knew that Charlie wasn't a murderer or a child abuser or anything like that. I could never ever fall for a murderer or child abuser. I don't have any time for such evil. But it did say in the paper that Charlie originally went to prison for armed robbery. After that, most of his crimes have been on the inside such as attacks on prison officers and taking a number of hostages. That didn't put me off, though, as I realise that there are two sides to everything. Eventually, I finished reading the newspaper and threw it in the dustbin.

In the evening, I didn't know what made me do it, but I went outside and retrieved the newspaper from the bin. I then turned to the page where Charles Bronson's photo was … and I looked at him. After a while, I wondered what on earth was happening to me. The same thought kept buzzing around my head: 'Who is this person and why am I looking at him like this?' The more I looked at the photo, the more I was drawn towards him. I just couldn't take my eyes off his photo that night.

Later – it must have been about midnight – I couldn't sleep, so I got up and came downstairs. 'This is crazy,' I thought to myself. 'I don't even know this man and he's completely overtaken my heart!' At that point, I just grabbed the newspaper and threw it back in the bin.

That night, I couldn't sleep a wink! I kept thinking about him all night and I couldn't work out what the hell was happening to me. Many times I resisted the temptation to go back to the bin and pull out the newspaper again, just to look at his face once more. I felt as though he was drawing me towards him like a magnet. I could almost smell his presence. It was pure madness! I had never felt like that before – within a day, this strange person had turned my whole life upside-down. I must also admit that it was one of the most wonderful feelings I've ever experienced.

The next day, I went to work. One of my colleagues said to me, 'You look too happy today ... have you won the lottery or something?'

'Yes,' I said, 'something like that!'

A few days went by, and others started to notice the joy in my face. I had a sort of glow that even my close friends started to notice as well.

Up until then, every night after Sami went to bed, I used to sit on my own and disappear in the darkness. Now, after seeing Charles's photo in the paper, I couldn't stop myself feeling infinitely happier, with less pain. Only God knew what was happening to me. It was as though this unknown person had brought some wonderful dreams into my empty existence, as though he had breathed new life into a half-dead corpse. Have you ever seen a plant dying without any water? When you water it again, it slowly comes back from the dead, renewed, refreshed. That's how I felt. It was amazing how a complete stranger had brought some happiness to my completely unconnected life.

A couple of months later, he was in the paper again, but this time it was in *Luton on Sunday*. As soon as I saw his photo again, a tingly shiver ran up my spine. I felt as though he was right there with me, in person. He just seemed extraordinarily close. I wanted to tell someone, but I didn't know how to express myself. For the first time in my life, I felt that I didn't have any control over my feelings. I was completely overtaken by some sort of invisible force. There was no doubt that I was falling in love with Charles, and I realised that it wasn't some kind of infatuation or anything. I've been through enough in life to know the difference between love and lust.

Another five to six months went by like that, without any change in my feelings for Charles. I found it increasingly hard to believe that, out of all the people in the world, I'd fallen for someone I'd never met or even seen with my own eyes. Perhaps the most amazing aspect of all this was that I hadn't just fallen for him when I saw his photo – there was much more to it than that. It was almost as though it was meant to be. At times, I even felt that there was something wrong with me, as I'm generally a very practical, realistic person.

There came a point where I said to myself, 'Get real ... stop thinking about Charles and start thinking about meeting someone and settling down.' So I started to concentrate on my work, dancing, Sami and other aspects of my life, so I could forget about Charles. I convinced myself that I needed to forget about him and I knew that I could do it if I put my mind to it. Who was he, anyway, and why should I feel so strongly about him?

I become more heavily involved at work. Because of the type of work we did at the women's centre, we had a lot of dealings with the Luton Police, such as making referrals and so on. One person I often dealt with a man who helped with work for local people.

We became friends, and slowly grew to like each other a little more than just friends. I still needed someone to love me, as I was trying desperately to get Charles out of my mind. So I started seeing him, and my Sami liked him as well. All the time, I tried my very best to erase all thoughts of Charles from my mind.

Peter and I had a good relationship for about six or seven

months. Then we started to have problems. I would say we cared for each other, but neither of us loved the other, and so our relationship wasn't very profound. It was also quite unbalanced – I put 100 per cent into the relationship and, like many Asian women, I gave and gave until there was nothing left to give. It's a wonderful quality to have, I think, but people can often find it difficult to deal with.

There were times when I used to get upset with him because he never said he loved me. Not once. I asked him a few times whether he even loved me a little bit. He never found it easy to talk about that, and he'd get all agitated for some reason. So I never forced him to reply directly. Then, the next day, he would phone me as usual and everything would be back to normal.

Can you believe that, for about six months, he never gave me his home number or address? I found that very strange. We had an argument one day over that, which prompted him to give me his contact details. But I never rang him or used his address, because I knew that he was worried about his family and friends finding out that he was seeing an Asian woman, and I was living in the same community where he worked.

A year went by like that, and I was getting progressively fed up with him. He wasn't making any effort towards our relationship at all. He never took Sami and me out anywhere or to his place; he always used to come to our house for a short while, then go home when it was dark. And he never wanted me to tell anyone about our relationship. Some of my friends said that he was a waste of time, that he was never going to marry me. And they all knew how hard I was trying with him. At times, they became really frustrated with me for being so naïve and not realising that he didn't want any future with me.

I should have seen the signs a bit earlier, I suppose. In two years, he only took Sami and me out five times – once in London, and four times to his house! Soon, even I could see that there was no way he was going to marry me or settle down. Still, being an Asian woman, I decided to give it my best shot. I must have cared about him more than I realised.

We had 'been together' for around two years, when strange things started to happen to me again. Charles reappeared! I just could not get him out of my mind. Slowly, my feelings for Charles were taking me over, and soon they would affect the relationship I was having. Whenever he tried to be close to me, I used to feel really guilty. I felt as though no other man had got the right to touch me apart from Charles. I felt as though I was his, and convinced myself that I was 100 per cent in love with him. It's difficult to explain just how good I felt for the first time in my life; I didn't care that my existing relationship was going down the drain.

So many times I felt like screaming and telling the world that I was in love! My whole life was beautiful. I'd never realised that love could transform such a grey life into something of such beauty. I actually thanked God for granting me such a wonderful experience. I truly felt in my heart that being in love with Charles was a kind of blessing from God himself. It may be unbelievable, but it's true.

But it wasn't all sweetness and light. I was frightened at the same time, in case my dream only remained just that – a dream. What if I never got to tell him? How would I find him? What if he was married? What if he was one of those men with girlfriends everywhere? Then what's going to happen? All sorts of questions raced through my mind.

So, in a way, I was trying to move forward in life but, at the same time, my feelings for Charles were getting in the way. Strange things used to happen to me sometimes at night when I was in a deep sleep. I used to wake up in the middle of the night and feel his presence close to me, and then I would look around me, as though he had been next to me just before I opened my eyes! Then I would just go back to sleep with a smile. That was a nice feeling of closeness. Before, all the nights had been so long but, after falling in love with Charles, the nights became too short. And it wasn't only the nights – one lifetime didn't seem enough to be in love with him. Of course, there were times when I said to myself, 'Enough is enough … this isn't realistic at all. I could seriously get hurt if he doesn't like me back.' But I continued to trust my instincts.

One day, as usual, the man I was seeing came to see me. He used to come around to see me every other day, straight from work. I used to cook for us regularly, and after dinner he used to spend some time with Sami and me. If we were lucky, he'd to stay 'til midnight, then go home.

That particular day, he came to see me, and Sami went to bed early. He was sitting very close to me and, eventually, we both started to get even closer. He hugged me very close, and I closed my eyes. When I opened them, I looked at him, as I wanted to kiss him, but I couldn't. I just could not bring myself to do that. I actually felt guilty as I was in love with Charles. I moved away from him straight away. He didn't make a comment at all.

That day, I was convinced that I could no longer carry on with the relationship as long as I had those feelings for Charles. I told myself that I should completely wipe this unknown person from my mind, or go to the doctor and get some help. I even made an appointment with my doctor, and actually went to the doctor's surgery, but I only got as far as the waiting room before coming back home. I just couldn't face the doctor; I thought he would think I was being silly and laugh at me.

After that day, I didn't hear from my friend for a week. I didn't know what to do. At one point, I thought of telling him the truth about Charles, and then maybe he would understand and help me return to reality. That is, if he really cared about me. Then, the next minute, I was wondering why I should call him. If he cared about me at all, then surely he would call me. Another three days went by, and still no call.

I can still remember that it was on millennium night when I phoned him and invited him to a night out in London, because that night was special to me. I was performing classical dance with my dance group in one of the Indian dinner-dance venues, so I wanted him to come with Sami and me. It was also the start of the millennium, a night when all couples would be together. He made an excuse saying that he couldn't come because he was working that night.

It was just another excuse. Perhaps he didn't want to be seen in public with me. From that day on, I never rang him, and he never tried to ring me. I lost my faith in him, and had little respect left for him.

After that, I decided to forget about him. I just thanked God my Sami didn't get attached to him, otherwise she would have been hurt and I can't have anyone hurting my Sami. I'm not a violent person, but I'd happily turn anywhere into a war zone if anybody ever did that.

Sami did miss my friend for a few days, but after that she was fine, and so another chapter of my life was over.

If I had the chance, I'd say to him, 'You never even said that you loved me. If you didn't have any feelings for me, then why the hell did you waste my time from the beginning? Do you remember when we went to London and we took some photos? You didn't even put your arms around me … straight away, I should have realised that you were embarrassed about being seen with me. My biggest mistake was to fall for someone like you.'

I was on my own again. Yes, what happened had hurt but, despite all that, I decided to concentrate on other aspects of my life. It was very hard at times, and I started to feel empty again. Mentally, I felt tired, very tired: tired of fighting, as though there was no end to what I was going through; I was missing Bangladesh as well; I was feeling homesick; I was missing my father and I wanted to be with my mother and my little brother. I used to cry a lot whenever I phoned them, saying, 'I want my father ... I've got nobody here.' My mother and brothers used to comfort me. But I couldn't get on a plane and see them – Nunu's family were still a realistic threat.

I guess my work and classical dance group kept me occupied. We all got on really well in the dance group. Amir Butt was the manager, as well as being the DJ. He was a prison officer, but managing the dance group and DJing was his hobby in his spare time. He was like a brother to me, and I got to know his wife and mother as well. Then there was Mala and Sabrina, who were more like sisters to me, as well as close friends. There were other really nice members of the group as well, and we had a lot of fun performing in different places.

One thing remained constant throughout all this – at the end of the day, no matter what I did, whom I was with or how much fun I had had, I just could not get Charles out of my mind. I didn't know what I could do to change my feelings for Charles and, although I tried, I found it impossible. The more I tried not to think about Charles, the more feelings I started to have.

It got to the point where I wondered whether I'd completely lost my mind one evening. It was my friend Sabrina's sister's birthday, and it was held in an Indian dinner-dance place in London, called Maya. At about 7.30pm, we all arrived outside the venue dressed up in very smart, traditional Asian outfits. Each of us looked a million dollars. As I walked towards the place, I could not believe what I saw – the white English doorman on security looked a lot like Charles Bronson. I nearly had a heart-attack there and then! Sabrina said, 'What's the matter with you? You look as though you've seen a ghost or something.'

'Yes, something like that!' I mumbled.

I could still see that doorman from our table once we'd all sat down. I couldn't help sneaking little glances at him over and over again. I thought to myself, 'What the hell is this? What the hell is happening to me?'

As the evening wore on, I was really enjoying myself, and then Sabrina and I took over the dance floor and danced away to the live Indian dance music. Then everybody joined us. For a moment, I just stopped dancing and kept on looking at the doorman while nobody was watching. He was just walking around the dance floor, fulfilling his duties and, as he walked towards me, I could hear my own heartbeat. I just stood there and looked at him. When he finally noticed that I was looking at him, he returned my gaze and smiled! I immediately hid behind Sabrina, as I felt really embarrassed.

By then, Sabrina had noticed what was going on, and she had got completely the wrong idea – she thought that I fancied him! I was dying to tell her the truth about Charles, but I just didn't know where to start. I knew that what I was doing – feeling attracted to the doorman because he looked like someone else – was wrong, but I didn't want to let that moment go; it was simply too precious.

The party carried on and then, at about 2.30am, I asked Sabrina to come with me so I could have a closer look at him. We both walked past him a few times, and by then he'd cottoned on to the fact that I liked him! I thought to myself, 'I've got to talk to him.'

At about 3.00am, the place started packing up, and the doorman was standing at the door saying goodbye to everyone. I wrote my number on a piece of paper, then, as we were walking away, I dropped it in front of him and said to him, 'I think you dropped something from your pocket!' After that, I just walked away. My friends couldn't believe what I'd done.

I got home with Sabrina, who was staying with me for a couple of days. She kept on asking me all kinds of questions about the doorman, but she was basically happy for me. I didn't talk much, got changed, washed my off make-up then went to bed. That night, I just couldn't sleep with so many thoughts racing around my head – I've fallen for that doorman only because he looks a little bit like Charles. What's going to happen tomorrow? I can't go around being attracted to people just because they are Charles Bronson lookalikes! People will think I've finally flipped!

The next day, I got a text message from him saying he liked me, too. I thought to myself, 'What the hell am I going to do now?' By lunchtime, he must have sent me seven or eight messages! Eventually, I sent him a couple of messages saying 'Hello' and 'How are you?' and that went on for a couple of days. Then he wanted to meet me. God help me, what am I supposed to do now?

I asked Sabrina's advice; what should I do, as I was certain now that I didn't want to go out with him. She was a little bit annoyed with me, saying that he seemed a nice man so why the hell wouldn't I give him a chance? As it turned out, he never contacted me back, so the decision was made for me. I felt as though God had intervened on my behalf, and I resolved – never again! I'd been really stupid to have got so obsessed.

While all this was happening in England, I kept in close touch with my family in Bangladesh. They were doing well financially; I was pleased that my hard work had paid off. My family's wellbeing was a top priority of mine, and I was always keen to make sure that they were all right. Personally, I have never wanted anything from them, except to love me. After everything that has happened, from when I was a little girl in Bangladesh to my divorce from Nunu, it warms my heart to hear what my mother has come to say of me: that I'm not only her daughter, I'm her son as well. This is her way of complimenting me because of how I've always been the backbone of my family, despite having to deal with my own problems.

What more do I need from my own mother? Nothing … absolutely nothing. The fact is, whatever I've done for my family –

and whatever I do in the future – I haven't done any of it for my mother to praise me. I've done it simply because it is part of our culture and my own responsibility towards my family. In our culture, we love and respect our parents after God. Believe me, you can't achieve anything in life without the blessing of your parents. So make sure you do your very best for your parents, especially when they are older and need your help the most.

Something that makes me feel sick is when I see old people being neglected by their own children. They have to live in old people's homes, while the sons and daughters enjoy nice, comfortable lives in their own houses. Many of these older people are the same parents who sacrificed so much all their lives to provide the best for their children, and look at the thanks they get.

I was watching one of the Indian digital television channels called Zee TV, when an advert came on with the message: 'Adopt a granny for only £3 a month.' I was furious! Whatever the reasons for older relatives to end up like this, it breaks my heart. Our values seem to be disappearing day by day, and only God knows where it will end.

I actually have a secret dream: one day, I want to set up some sort of network in Bangladesh to help the hundreds of thousands of neglected, elderly mothers and fathers. I want to be their daughter as well as their son, and give them the love they deserve. I know I have so much love to give, and I believe I can make some sort of a difference in their lives, as young children and our elderly are the most vulnerable people in our society. I do hope I have the ability to do something like this, as it would be an honour. In fact, it seems to me that we all have a moral responsibility to ensure that it happens.

After I'd arrived in England, and I found out that many elderly people in England live in old people's homes, I used to feel really sad about it. Now, I'm not criticising Western culture, please don't get me wrong. I do know that the elderly are well looked after in such places most of the time, and that most of them get regular visits, but

I personally believe that an aged parent's place is in the family home, not in an institution. Sometimes, when I go out to do my shopping and see an elderly person struggling to carry a shopping bag, it makes me feel really sad. With God's help, I do intend to do all I can to repay some of the sacrifices made by our older generation.

12 CONTACT

It was in December 1998 when I first saw that photo of Charles in the paper; it was now December 2001. I'd been in love with Charles Bronson for three years! Three long years! I realised that I finally had to do something. I wanted to find Charles and tell him how I felt towards him.

I had no idea of how or where to start looking for him, so I approached Amir, our dance group manager, who was also a prison officer. I thought that he would know where Charles might be, as I had no idea of how to negotiate the prison system. I didn't feel confident enough to tell Amir the truth, so I lied to him, saying, 'I know this woman in Luton ... she was asking me to find out from you which prison Charles Bronson is in ...'

Amir just looked at me as though I'd lost my mind! When he'd recovered his composure, he said, 'Ask that silly woman what she wants his address for ... He's a nutcase!'

'OK,' I thought, 'I get the message.' I didn't want to push it any further with Amir, so the next day, after a lot of thinking, I picked up the phone, dialled 192 and spoke to someone at directory enquiries. 'How do I go about finding out which prison a particular inmate is in?' I asked, and I was given the number for the Prisoner Location Service.

I rang them that day and spoke to a nice lady, who said she couldn't just give me Charles's address or his prison number, she had to ask his permission first. I was happy with that, so I wrote to her that day, as I had to make my request in writing. I was really excited, as it was my first official step towards Charles.

A week went by with no reply from the Prisoner Location Service. I rang them again, but they said that, because it was Christmas, my request might take a little longer to process.

On 24 December, Sabrina invited Sami and me to her place. We had some classical dance shows booked as well in the run-up to the New Year, so I went to London for the holiday period. On 28 December, a group of us were invited to an Asian family party. While I was there, I got talking to a friend of ours, and we soon ended up talking about Charles. I asked him if he knew which prison he was in. He said he didn't know much about Charles, but that there was a website about him. Well, that did it! I made up an excuse to Sabrina and left the party with my friend, to use his computer and get on to the Internet.

Fortunately, this friend and his wife were very generous people, so, when we arrived at their house at about 9.30pm, I put Sami to bed, made a cup of tea for myself then sat down in front of the computer.

I clicked on to the website and immediately I saw his face. My God, that was the very first time I'd ever seen a proper photo of him. I could hear my own heartbeat, and it seemed as if the whole planet had stopped turning for a moment. I sat back down on the sofa and looked at his photo, and thought to myself, 'He's the one for me.' I didn't need to know anything else about him.

I read through some information about him, such as why he was in prison and how badly he had been treated. That night, I was on that website until 2.30am! Then I printed out some of his photos to take with me. I just couldn't sleep that night, smiling and thinking so many things. I must have had only a couple of hours' sleep, but the following morning I still had a glow on my face from the night before.

At about midday, I went back to Sabrina's place, as we had a dance show as well that night. I was so happy that day that I decided to tell Sabrina everything after the show. When I was performing that night, I swear to God that I have never experienced so much joy while dancing. Charles infused my mind, heart, body and soul, and was my inspiration for every dance movement. I could feel him in the music. It was a beautiful experience I'll never forget.

After the show, I told Sabrina everything. She didn't know how to react. One minute she was saying that I was insane, and the next she was hugging me, saying she was so happy for me. I said to her, 'I waited three years for this! Now I want to write to him and tell him how I feel. If he doesn't like me back, then it's my bad luck ... but if he likes me, then I'll be the luckiest woman alive to have found love like this.' She was happy for me, I guess, but advised me not to get my hopes up too high, as I could get hurt if he didn't want to contact me.

The following day, I came back home, and I could not believe my eyes when I saw a letter from the Prisoner Location Service. The first thing I did was kiss the letter. Then I opened it ... and found Charles's address and prison number.

I didn't waste any time. I decided to write a letter to Charles that night, and thought to myself that it didn't matter if he didn't want to take things any further. At least telling him how I felt would make me feel better. Perhaps then I could move on with my life.

I started the letter and, once I'd got going, the rest was easy. I told him everything – who I was, about my Sami, where I came from, my work, dance, and how I'd ruined one or two relationships because I couldn't get him out of my mind. Basically, I didn't miss out a thing! I even included my home and mobile phone numbers and address, as well as a photo of myself, so he could see me with his own eyes. I wrote on the back of the photo, 'I'm not trying to impress you by sending you the photo, I just want you to see the person behind this letter.' I didn't want to have any regrets after posting the letter.

Once I'd sent the letter, I told myself that, whatever happened, at least I could get on with my life. That night, I slept like a baby, no tension, nothing, and smiled as I thought about Charles receiving my letter the next day. For the first time, he would know my feelings for him. It felt like being in heaven just thinking about that.

The next day, I had another dance show in London, so I had to be there. Sami and I came back home late that night and I was so tired I switched off my mobile and home phone, as I didn't want to be disturbed by anyone.

The following morning, my entire life changed! I got up very late because of all the dance shows and partying I'd been doing. At about 9.30am, I heard the postman drop a few letters through the letterbox, so I staggered down to pick them up. There was a postcard among them, and a letter, with the same postmarks … and then it clicked. They were from Charles. This time, my heart must have stopped beating for real! I was standing by the door with his letter and card, just staring at them, hardly daring to move, just feeling the weight of them, and then I realised that I should read them!

I sat down and read the postcard first, in which he wrote that he'd tried to call me a few times but my phone was switched off.

Then I opened the letter. To start with, he asked why a nice woman like myself would want to get involved with someone like him. Then he described himself for a while, and then he asked some general questions about what went wrong in my marriage and so on. He talked about Sami as well, and wondered if, the next time I wrote, I'd mind sending a close-up photo of myself. I knew from that that he definitely liked me! Still, I didn't want to get my hopes up, and I was really annoyed with myself for having switched off my mobile.

The next day, I went to work as usual. During the day, my mobile rang, and it turned out to be somebody called Mr Khan. He said in a very formal voice, 'I'm Charles Bronson's solicitor … Charlie told me to tell you that he has been trying to call you but missed you, but he will call you very soon. Look, I've only phoned you because Charlie asked me to; if you had been just anybody, I wouldn't have rung.'

I thought that he sounded very important. Most of all, I was very surprised that Charles had been trying to get hold of me on the phone. I then decided to take a few days off work and stay at home in case he rang me on my home number. I also kept the mobile switched on and placed it right beside me. Well, I wasn't going to take any more chances, was I?

Thursday and Friday came and went with no phone calls, and on Friday night I fell asleep downstairs on the sofa as I was very tired. Then at 9.00am on Saturday morning, the phone rang. I woke up wondering who the hell it was phoning me at that time of the morning. I answered the phone.

'Is it Saira?' a very deep, sexy voice asked.

'Yes,' I said, still half-asleep.

'It's Charlie here,' the voice said, 'you wrote to me.'

I thought, yeah, right, some idiot's winding me up. Then he said, 'Saira, you took three years to come to me!' and that's when I knew straight away that it could be no one else but Charles. We spoke for about 15 minutes, and he asked to speak to Sami as well.

It was really strange – we were talking as though we'd known each other for ages. Neither of us felt awkward, even though we were speaking for the first time. I caught myself wondering whether this was actually happening or was I dreaming? I was actually speaking to the man I'd been in love with for three years.

'Saira,' he said, 'a lot of people write to me, but when I received your letter there was something special about it. I don't know what it was, but I'll find out soon.'

When he said that, I felt in my heart that he felt the same as me, but I didn't say anything to him. I wanted to wait and see if he actually felt the same or not.

I decided to tell my Sami all about Charles, but I wasn't sure how she would take it. When I explained everything about Charles and me to her, Sami was very happy. She thought about things for a bit, and said, 'Mum, do you think he will be my dad one day?' I looked at my Sami's little face and saw the hope written all over it. All I said was, 'Let's see what happens. As much as I would love it to be like that, we have to wait and see what happens.'

I sent Charles another letter with some photos of Sami and me and, the next day, I received another letter from Charles. In this second letter, I could see clearly that he liked me a lot. What really struck me was when he wrote, 'Saira, I feel as though I've been drawn towards you since I received your first letter, as it was very powerful. It's as though I've got no choice but to write to you.' After reading that, I felt for the first time that we were meant to be together; nothing more and nothing less.

We then wrote to each other every single day, and Charles phoned me every week. Before we knew it, we had become very close to one another, so close, in fact, that we weren't really two people any more, we were almost like one soul. I couldn't believe that I had actually found such a perfect love after such a lifetime of pain.

Over the first two weeks of getting to know each other, we both noticed that there was so much we had in common – our thoughts, dreams, sadness, pain – the list was endless. What linked us particularly was the pain we had both suffered – of course, our experiences had been vastly different, but pain is pain.

I wanted to know everything he'd been through, so he sent me his book *Bronson*. It was very hard for me to read, because of all the hardship he had been through in his prison life. I was amazed that he'd managed to survive all those years. My own pain and sadness felt trivial compared to some of the horrifying treatment the prison service had inflicted upon him. I was able to comfort him in my letters and on the phone, and I told him that, little by little, I'd take away all his pain one day. We were together now, so we could fight together now and get him out of prison.

Charles also wanted to know all about my past, especially all the hardship I'd been through. I must admit, he took away most of my pain and replaced it with a great deal of love. I didn't care what happened now, because I'd found love, we'd found each other, and we'd both found the happiness we'd been looking for all our lives.

Three weeks later, Charles said to me that he wanted to see me as soon as possible. I felt exactly the same. But I just couldn't jump in a taxi and go to see him. I had to go through a police check, which is the normal procedure if you want to visit any inmate in prison. The whole process usually takes somewhere between one and two months. So I filled in all the necessary forms, and then I just had to wait to be granted a visit. That wait seemed like a lifetime, as we were dying to see each other.

One day on the phone, he said to me, 'Saira, do you know that we will get married one day as well?'

I put my hand over my heart and said, 'How did you know that I feel exactly the same?' He must have read my mind.

Sami and Charles started to write to each other as well, and they spoke to each other regularly on the phone. The two of them got on very well, and it seemed as though a natural father–daughter bond developed between them. I was very pleased with that. Everyone knows that you can't force a child to like or love someone, so, as far as I was concerned, it was another miracle that

Sami became close to him, giving me even more reason to believe that God had planned all this for me.

With every letter, Charles would also include his artwork. What a wonderful, talented artist he is. His drawings are amazing, usually expressing his feelings, his life inside the prison, his past and the people in his life. His art became a part of our lives. If we didn't get a drawing with a letter, Sami and I both felt that there was something missing!

But Charles is not just an artist, he is a poet as well, writing the most beautiful poems for us. No one had ever done anything as nice as that. He was such a one-off, he was unlike anyone I'd ever known, and most of all he was my heart and soul. Day by day, we fulfilled each other's needs spiritually, paving the way for our dream of being together forever.

A couple of months went by, and our relationship grew from strength to strength. I just thanked God every day for giving me such a gift of love. For the first time, I admitted to myself that it had been worth all the nightmares I'd been through. I had found someone priceless, so who needed anything else? Out of all the men out there, I had found my love in prison.

By then, all my friends had found out about Charles and me. Most of them couldn't understand how I could possibly feel like this, and thought that a relatively intelligent woman like myself had finally gone insane! I thought I'd give them some time to get used to the idea. Once they got to know the truth about Charles, they would understand him better. Some of my friends actually tried to put me off Charlie by saying frightening things about him. They said that I'd become a victim of his violence and anger one day! But they didn't know me. I don't fear anyone, except myself.

I went to work one morning as usual, and told one of my colleagues about Charles as I was so happy. I think she was shocked, rather than surprised. Her first reaction was, 'Oh ... Now it's a criminal then?' I realised then that most of them would take a great deal of convincing to get them on my side. I thought it was a shame that people could be judged so quickly without knowing anything about them.

When I told Charles about the reaction I was getting at work, he asked me whether I wanted to keep our relationship a secret, or would I mind if people knew about it? The reason he asked was because the media followed his activities from time to time, so sooner or later they would find out about me as well. Then, as usual, they would write whatever they liked.

I told Charles that I wanted to keep our relationship private for the time being, simply because it was nobody else's business. I was also an Asian woman, and I had never dealt with the media, so I would find that very difficult. It was an issue we were both a bit worried about. I also had to bear in mind that, when the Asian community found out, I knew that they would make my life difficult, especially in Luton, as there are so many Asians living there.

To most Asian people, seeing my photo in the newspaper would be bad enough; they wouldn't even read the story. Just seeing my photo in the paper would be enough to help them make up their minds about me. And people also believed everything they read, as if it was the gospel truth. Sad, but that's the reality. So we both left it at that and waited to see what happened.

Eventually, Charles introduced me to one of his friends, Tracey Pearce, someone whom he looked upon as his sister, who lived with her boyfriend and two children in Hemel Hempstead. She rang me one day for the first time and introduced herself as Charles Bronson's personal secretary. When I spoke to her, she seemed a very nice woman; we got on very well. In our first conversation, she told me all about Charles and what was happening with his legal situation. I was very happy to meet a nice lady like her; I respected her because she was Charles's friend.

As time ticked on, Charles and I just couldn't wait to see each other. We were really excited, and very happy. One morning, I had a letter from the police saying that they would like to come and see me for an interview that was all part of the permission process. A week later, a police intelligence officer came to see me at my house. I knew that they would eventually allow me to see Charles, because I do not have any criminal record, and we were in a relationship and planning to get married.

The day the police officer came to interview me, Tracey turned up at the same time, along with her boyfriend, but I didn't mind them staying with me while the officer was conducting the interviewing. Once he'd finished, the officer left, saying he would let me know very soon if they would pass me or not. Tracey and her boyfriend assured me that there would be no problem with the outcome, and told me not to worry. We talked for hours about Charles, which was lovely, and I gave Tracey a gold bangle and a pair of earrings as a gift, as a token of respect from Sami and me. We believe, as part of our Bangladeshi heritage, that, when a special guest comes to your house, you should honour them with a small gift.

The next day, Charles told me, 'Saira, you can trust Tracey like your own sister, as I treat her like a sister as well. She won't do us any harm. So, if you have any problems, always tell Tracey, as I asked her to look out for Sami and you. Always depend on her and have faith in her.' I felt that was very nice of Charles to think of us. From that day, I started to treat Tracey like my own sister, and I used to tell people, 'Hey, I've got a sister now!'

A week later, I found out that I had passed the police check to go and visit Charles. He was absolutely delighted, and really excited as well. Who says dreams don't come true?

13 MEETING OF MINDS

We booked my visit for 4 March 2001; I now had only two weeks to prepare myself! We both decided that, for the first time, I'd visit him on my own, because we weren't sure how Sami would feel going through the security check inside the prison. So we decided that Sami would accompany me on my second visit, as Charles saw Sami and me as equally important.

God, that two weeks to us was like two months ... or two years! Charles wanted to know what I would wear, but I wanted him to choose, so I sent him some photos of some options. Then he told me that he was 200 per cent sure that he was in love with me as well. I lost count how many times I read that part of his letter: 'Saira, I love you ...' I can't begin to express how I'd been dying to hear that from him.

After I'd read that in his letter, he phoned me that day as well, and repeated it to me over the phone. I wanted to hear that again and again and, throughout the following two weeks, we both talked about planning the wedding. I have no words to describe how happy I was. He said to me, 'Saira, you started off loving me, now I feel as though I love you more than anything else. I even love your little Sami as my own child.'

What more did I need? Nothing. My Sami even wrote to him and asked him if she could call him 'Dad'. He wrote back, saying, 'Saira, that put a lump in my throat! I felt so special.' Then he wrote to Sami, 'Yes, of course you can call me Dad.'

Honestly, I felt that Charles had given Sami something so special, that even I hadn't been able to give her for the previous ten years. The fact is, no matter how much I love my Sami, whatever I did for her, I could never give her a father's love. Now I can say my Sami has got her father; Nunu was never a father to her, and never will be.

One morning, I went to work as usual, and one of my colleagues knocked on my door and said there was a message for me from Charles. He phoned my work every now and then. When I looked at my colleague's face, I could sense the disapproval at Charles ringing the office, but I kept quiet.

Then, at about lunchtime, I had an hour's break, so I went to attend my hairdresser's appointment. While I was making my way there, I had a strange feeling that I was being followed. Then, while I was sitting in the hairdresser's, I had a call from a woman who said, 'Hello, Saira, how are you? Where are you at the moment?'

I asked her who she was. She said she was from the *Daily Mail* newspaper and wanted to speak to me about Charles's and my relationship. I told her in a very polite way that I wouldn't be able to make any comment, and with that I switched off my mobile.

After I left the hairdresser's, I went straight back to the office. I didn't know what the hell to do; I was becoming more frightened and confused. My colleague then said, 'Saira, a woman was looking for you after you left the office.' I knew immediately which woman she was talking about. I thought, 'I'm finished!' I was really frightened, as I'd never spoken to anybody from the media before, and I didn't know what to expect.

I felt really confused and anxious, so I took the afternoon off and came home in a taxi and locked the door. Then my next-door neighbour came over and said, 'Saira, some people were knocking on your door!'

What I couldn't understand was how they had got hold of my phone numbers and address. The only people who had my address and numbers were my close friends, so I couldn't work it out at all.

At 3.15pm, I left the house to pick up Sami from school as usual. As soon as I stepped out of my front door, I noticed that a woman and a man were sitting in a car opposite my house taking photos of me. It was obvious to me that she was the same reporter from the *Daily Mail*. Without looking at them, I nervously started to walk as fast as I could. As soon as I reached the end of our road, they parked their car in front of me and started to walk behind me, and then eventually they caught up with me. The reporter stopped me and pointed her microphone at me, while the photographer was snapping away at me. She immediately fired a string of questions at me, along the lines of: if I was a respectable Asian woman, why was I marrying a dangerous inmate such as Charles? What had made me fall in love with him in the first place? Didn't I fear his violent reputation in prison? I can't remember what else she asked me.

But I just said politely, 'Please go ... I do not wish to make any comment,' and I kept on repeating that until the reporter and her sidekick left me. The most embarrassing thing was that, while they were interviewing me in the street with their microphone and camera, all the Asian onlookers were staring at me and laughing, wondering at the same time why on earth the reporters were talking to me anyway.

Somehow I reached the school gate, and went into the main office to pick up Sami because, whenever a parent was late, the children would wait inside the building. When I reached the school's main reception area, I saw the same reporter going into the headteacher's office. It was obvious that it had something to do with me.

I started to panic. I didn't know what to do, but I grabbed one of the teachers and told her that I wanted to see the headteacher, who eventually came out to see me. I told her what had happened out on the street, and felt I had to tell her about Charles's and my relationship as well. I didn't want to explain things in detail, simply because it was none of her business, but I reasoned that she should know as much as possible, as it was now affecting the school and Sami. She told me that the *Daily Mail* reporter had given her some old newspaper cuttings regarding Charles's notoriety, and she showed them to me.

I then told her that I was aware of Charles's past and, yes, it was true that Sami and I loved him. I added that our relationship was also nobody's business but ours, so therefore I didn't have to justify it to anybody. The headteacher looked at me as though I'd completely lost my mind! She just couldn't understand my point of view.

That attitude towards me was true not only of the headteacher, but also a lot of my friends. People mainly asked me whether I was afraid of him. Didn't he frighten me? I told them, no, I wasn't afraid. Charlie is not a monster of a killer, rapist or a child-abuser. He was originally sent to prison for armed robbery, then, while serving his prison sentence, he became violent towards the prison guards, for various reasons. His past violence has purely been aimed at the prison services, not at anybody outside, or any women or children.

After the incident in the street, I came back home with Sami from her school. Then I phoned Tracey, telling her everything that had happened. She suggested that, if I did a story with a newspaper about our relationship, after that they would leave me alone. She told me that I should think about that.

Now I was even more confused! I thought about it all night, and then I thought that I'd talk it all through with Charles the next day when he phoned. But very early the next morning, Tracey rang me and said that the *Daily Mail* had done the story already! 'I'm dead now,' I thought.

That day, I didn't want go into work, so I took the day off. I went to the corner shop and bought the paper. As I was looking through it, at first I didn't even recognise my own photo! I was covered with snow. I nearly had a heart-attack. Obviously, the day before, when the photographer had been taking photos of me, it had been snowing. I looked like I'd just got out of a bubble bath with my coat on! It was frightening! And I knew that, as I was reading the story, so were ten of thousands of people all over Luton.

Later on that day, when Charles phoned, I told him all about it. I also told him what Tracey had suggested as well. We decided eventually that I'd do one story with one of the papers through Tracey, since she had been handling Charles's media campaigning, and she knew some of the people from the media very well. So she organised an interview for me with the *Sunday Express*, and I hoped that after doing one story everything would be all right.

To take my mind off the media interest, I reminded myself that there were only three days left 'til the big day – my visit. Tracey rang me and said that she was coming with me as well, plus her boyfriend. I was fine with that.

The big day, 4 March, dawned. The night before, we had had some very bad news; Charles's brother had died in Australia from cancer. I felt really bad for Charles, who had been in a prison cell all by himself when he heard that his brother had died thousands of miles away. Life can be very cruel at times. I didn't know what to do to help, and then, in the morning, Charles rang me. I asked him if he still wanted me to come to visit him.

'Babe,' he said, 'I knew long ago my brother was going to die. It's all fate that my brother died yesterday and I'm seeing you for the first time today. To me, it's like I lost a brother but I'm getting a loving wife today.'

I was in tears when he said that; he'd called me his wife before he had even married me.

I was so excited on the morning of my first visit to Charles, and Sami was excited as well. I wore a black dress with little white flowers on it, and black trousers, which he'd chosen earlier from the photos. I arrived at Woodhill Prison in Milton Keynes at 12.30pm with Tracey and her boyfriend, bursting with anticipation. It was strange, but I wasn't nervous at all; in fact, I felt as though I was going to visit my husband after a long time of being apart.

Eventually, at about 2.00pm, we were taken through the security check, which involved showing our passports and driving licences, and then we went through another security cordon in which we had to take off our shoes, watches, scarf – any accessories like that – and hand them in for scanning. Then, one by one, the female officer ran a metal detector over us from head to toe. After that, we had to open our mouths for a further examination.

Two prison guards then escorted us to the unit where they kept my soulmate. As each step took me closer to him, I felt this warm glow all over me. We must have walked for five minutes but to me it felt like half-an-hour.

As we got closer to the unit, Charles shouted through the grille of his basement cell. When I heard his voice, my heart skipped a beat. Then they brought him through a door at one end of the visiting room, while we waited to be let through ours. One of the guards commented that he was surprised that I wasn't nervous at all.

Finally, our door was unlocked and I walked in first. As I walked towards Charles, he walked towards me. As we met, before we did anything else, we just put our arms around each other. He held me in his arms so closely, I just wanted to melt into him. Then we both looked at each other and smiled, and then he kissed me on my lips.

To be honest, I didn't expect that at all. I just thought that when he met me he might just give me a kiss on my cheek or something. It was nice to have a kiss on the lips and get a great big hug. It's hard to explain, but I felt as though his presence lit up the entire room. He had this glow on his face and skin; he almost looked like an angel sent only for me. I have never seen that sort of glow on anyone in my life before, as if the whole room was bathed in it. Who says that there isn't a light at the end of the tunnel?

Then we all sat down at a very small table in the middle of the room, with three chairs on our side but only one chair on his. There were about eight prison guards in the room sitting quite a distance from us, and there were two or three cameras in the room as well. One was trained on us right above our heads. Woodhill was a maximum-security prison, and Charles was a high-risk prisoner, so I suppose this was just normal procedure.

Throughout the visit, Charles and I sat there holding hands. He said, 'Well, Saira, finally we meet!' God, he looked so happy. I just couldn't stop looking at him and thinking that here was my heartbeat, my love, my whole life was right in front of my eyes. I wanted to talk openly, but Tracey and her boyfriend were there as well, so that was a little bit difficult for both of us.

At times, he talked to Tracey but still looked at me, smiling. When he wasn't looking, I kept on sneaking glances at his hairy chest. He had lots and lots of hair on his chest and I loved it. I personally think men don't really look like real men without any hair on their chest.

Two hours later, the visit was over and we had to leave. Naturally, I didn't want to leave him, and felt quite sad that our first 'date' had to end like this.

After we left the prison, I didn't speak at all on the way home; I just allowed all my thoughts to wash over me. I had such a mixture of feelings to deal with – I'd actually got to meet the man I'd loved for three years; he loved me as much as I loved him, and then I had to leave him there.

When I got back, the first thing I did was pick up Sami from the childminder. She couldn't stop asking me questions about her dad. I told her everything, and she listened to it all with a big smile on her face.

Soon afterwards, we arranged another visit as Charles wanted to see Sami, and she was desperate to meet him. 'I'm going to see my dad,' she'd been telling everyone at school and, as her mother, I couldn't have been happier hearing my own child saying that, especially since she had never had a real dad to love her and care for her.

On the day of the visit, Sami was so excitable. I'd never seen her that happy. As she walked into the visiting room, she immediately went to hug her dad. And then, once we'd all sat down, father and daughter didn't stop talking. One minute she was talking to him, the next she was trying to pull his long moustache, and then she'd have a close inspection of his shaved head. I was simply bursting with pride and happiness to see the two of them getting on so well.

14 PUBLIC PROPERTY

When you dream, try and catch hold of it and, if you do, then never let it go. We felt as if we never wanted to let go of each other. Charles often said to me, 'Saira, never let go of what we have ... to let go would be the end of everything.' I used to think to myself, How could I let go of my heartbeat? That's how much he meant to me. He honestly was a part of me, and I was a part of him.

We started to talk about our wedding, which just felt right. We both knew very well that we were doing exactly the right thing. We weren't into seeing each other for seven years then getting married. Some people stay together for 20 years and still don't know each other well. With us, we felt as though we'd known each other for years and years. All we needed to do was to get married.

As we started planning our wedding, the media interest started to become quite intense. It was particularly difficult for someone like me to handle, who hadn't been born or brought up in England. I'm just a typical Bangladeshi woman, who's adapting as best she can to a Western lifestyle. Tracey advised me to go along with the publicity demands as she had convinced me that I was ultimately helping Charles's cause. However I found it very hard to cope with the pressure of dealing with the press.

Of course, someone in Charles's position needs all the good publicity he can get, as he is in an extraordinary situation. I thought, of course, that, if I could possibly contribute to any of that positive publicity, I would. However I was tired of saying the same things over and over again. In the end, I just decided to let people write whatever they liked. My only priority was Sami and my future husband, nothing else.

Things weren't going particularly well at my workplace either, because my colleagues and managers weren't happy with all the publicity, as they had to consider the centre's reputation. I still don't understand how my personal matters could be linked to my work, but that's what happened. Despite all that, I tried to keep my head down and get on with my job as efficiently as possible, because in only a month's time there would be a full-time job available at the centre, and there was no way I was going to let that chance slip away. At that time, I was the only qualified candidate at the centre, and everyone knew that.

My worst nightmare occurred when I got to work one morning. I arrived in the office as normal and, as I walked in, I felt that the atmosphere wasn't quite right. It wasn't the day for our management team meeting, but they were all in the middle of a meeting anyway. I tried not to take any notice of that, and then one of the team came and asked me to join the meeting. I assumed that it would simply be related to some aspect of the work that we were doing, but I soon discovered that the subject of the meeting was me!

In the room were eight members of the management team, and they told me that they had come to the conclusion that it would be best for the centre and myself if I left work for up to 12 weeks. Their reasons were directly related to the publicity that I and the centre had received, and the fact that potential clients might not want to use the centre if they found out the stories surrounding a particular member of staff. They added that they couldn't dismiss the fact that the centre was a referral agency for victims of domestic violence, and that Charles had a particular history of violence.

I couldn't believe what I was hearing! And, as I listened to their pathetic reasoning, I got more and more angry and upset. I tried to convey my point of view as forcefully as I could, but that didn't get me very far, as the management team had made its decision ... and that was final.

It's true to say that not everyone on that management team thought that the decision was right. There were some colleagues who would have tried to find a better compromise round the problem, because they valued the work I'd done and what I could do in the future, but they were too few and could not speak up on my behalf.

I was also extremely bitter over the way I was thrown out of my job, one that I loved, like an unwanted nuisance. There was little acknowledgement of the good work I'd done, or any sign of regret from certain colleagues that this had to happen. I was particularly hurt by the general attitude among them that I shouldn't be marrying a convicted armed robber, who has used violence in the past to achieve his ends. One colleague even said to me, 'Saira, you don't know what you are doing. You will realise it the day he gets violent with you and strangles you to death!'

This showed a complete misunderstanding of Charles, and our relationship. As I have already said, Charles's violence in the past has only ever been directed at the prison services, *never* at women and children. He has a deep love and respect for the innocent and vulnerable in our society. It was really sad to see that many of my friends and colleagues were swallowing everything they read in the tabloids hook, line and sinker, rather than trusting my judgement and being happy for me.

What's done was done. Even though I'd lost my job, I tried not to let that get me down. Why should I? I'd found happiness, and I was not going to let that disappear for anyone or anything. Of course, I would miss my job, as it had become like my second home. But I would survive.

My situation then went from bad to worse. Life started to become a great deal more complicated in Luton for us, as, by then, the entire local Asian population knew about us from reading stories in the newspapers or watching items about me on the local television news.

Many of the Asian children started bullying Sami at school, but very little was done by the teachers to help. Fortunately, Sami can be a tough kid, and she was a green belt in karate at the time. She was quietly confident, too, so she never let the bullying get to her.

One day, she was talking to her dad about school, when Charles said, 'Sami, I'm sorry you are getting problems at school because of me.'

'It's OK, Dad,' she replied. 'I only lost 12 friends to get a dad!'

'That's my girl!' Charles said, laughing.

Sami had visited her dad many times by then. Whenever I saw Sami and her dad together, they were my moments of pure happiness and satisfaction. I got so much joy from seeing the two of them sharing something so special.

As if losing my job wasn't enough, I was thrown out of my dance group as well. As I mentioned earlier, the man who was managing the dance group was a prison officer, and, when he found out about me getting married to Charles, he didn't want anything to do with me. I was really shocked. I couldn't help thinking what a lot of double standards there were surrounding all of this. I wasn't expecting that from anyone in the group at all, as we all seemed very close, like one big family.

After being upset for a day or two, I told myself that what had happened had happened for a good reason. At least now I knew that they had actually done me a favour. They could go to hell now, as far as I was concerned. I'd also lost all the dance contacts I'd made while I was with the group, as I was performing all over the place at the time, but, I still had the most precious thing of all in my life after Sami – Charles.

I still gave all my so-called friends some time to understand me; I thought, after a while, when they got to understand Charles better, they would be all right. But I was wrong. One day, I got really fed up when one of them said that Charles was only using me for publicity. I lost my temper and told all of them to get out of my life if they weren't going to respect or understand him. It made me feel good, too. Another bunch of idiots had been cleaned out of my life for good! Who needs them? I don't. All my life, I'd lived according to other people's expectations, and now I wanted to live and dedicate my life to my future husband and daughter, just like any other Bangladeshi woman.

As time went by, I continued to get hassle from various sectors of the Asian community. I couldn't get out of the house without some young men throwing insults at me, and I even had young women from college throwing things at me, or trying to push me off the pavement as they walked past. Sometimes, the idiots used to drive past and shout obscenities in front of my little girl. If you've ever had that sort of treatment, only then can you really understand just how hurtful and upsetting it can be. Verbal abuse is something that you don't forget very easily.

If I had a chance to speak to some of those young people who abused me, I'd ask them to think about how they'd feel if their mother, sister or cousin were treated like that. Would they be happy with that knowledge? Do they think that's acceptable?

As I looked at those young men, I thought of my baby brother back in Bangladesh, who would now be 22, and I felt so insulted that they were around the same age, and supposedly had similar values, but chose to behave in this way.

These young people are our future, and I sincerely hope that they are capable of seeing how being more tolerant and accepting makes for a better society.

This constant interest in my private affairs, and the hassle we got because of it, made me feel as though I was being pushed into a corner, and I was defenceless to do anything about it. Where were all those high-minded people when I was struggling day after day to survive on my own with a small child in a foreign country? Did anyone lift a finger to help me then, when I needed the community's support?

I think I know why they behaved like that with me. I am a very simple-looking person. When I go out, I always dress in a very plain way. I generally wear Asian clothes – a long top and trousers with a scarf around my neck. I never use any make-up, only a little bit of lipstick every now and then. Then I just look ahead as I walk down the street. I don't speak to anybody, I only concentrate on where I am going. Of course, if I meet somebody I know, I'll stop to say hello or have a chat. So, that is me in a nutshell, simple Saira walking along the street. Yes, I do dress up whenever there is a special occasion, but those instances are few and far between.

I couldn't help wondering if the people in Luton would have harassed me if my image had been different. If I had dressed in the best modern clothes, with lots of make-up, and had an attitude to match, or hired one or two bodyguards to walk alongside me, maybe people would have thought for a second before throwing abuse at me. I could have done that ... but why should I? That wouldn't have been my style. Why should I show off? And it wouldn't make any difference in my mind whether I was marrying Charles Bronson or Prince Charles! I would have to lose all my self-respect to change my image or behaviour just because my circumstances had changed. I am who I am and that's how I want to remain. Because I would never lose my self-respect for anybody. I'd never let anybody take away my sanity again. After all, it is my dignity and my sanity that gives me the recognition of my individuality.

So there I was fighting obstacles again, but this time I was fighting for love, and I would do it all over again for love. I tried to overcome every hurdle to hold on to my dream. Charles and I knew that, from the beginning, we would have many problems along the way, and he explained that there would be plenty of ill-wishers trying their best to split us up. I knew that I would have to be extra strong to resist their malicious intentions.

In the meantime I felt that the press I was doing was not working out the way I would have liked for Charlie. Tracey and I didn't see eye to eye on a number of issues.

I increasingly felt that I was being portrayed as a stupid dupe, someone who was really nothing more than a big joke whom people could laugh at over their Cornflakes. As I've said before, I wasn't against publicity per se; I would have done absolutely anything to help Charles, as he was my heart and soul. I just thought that the publicity I was doing did more harm than good.

Poor Charles, what could he do while he was locked up? God knows how he put up with some of those people year after year. He can't pick up the phone and solve problems when they occur, as he isn't allowed a phone whenever he likes.

As far as the money was concerned, there was a great deal of speculation over how much I and others were making out of all the publicity. Let me make it perfectly clear – I never took my cut. Occasionally, Tracey paid for my taxi fare to her house for interviews or meetings, and then, as my wedding approached, I took £400 from her to cover some costs; I had very little choice about that at the time. But that is all I ever took out of any publicity.

So as to avoid any confusion, that is something I'm not bitter about at all – I'm not complaining, as that was a decision I made from the beginning. I had also made it 100 per cent clear to Charles that I did not wish to touch any publicity money. I suggested, whenever the question of money came up, that the money should be given to charity.

It has been insulting to say the least to hear some people accusing me of making money out of my relationship with Charles. And, if there is still doubt, I give my full permission to any official investigator to ask any of the media organisations whether they paid me anything for talking to them. They will soon discover that I have been paid nothing, and neither has Charles, because while he is in prison he is not allowed to profit in any way. Knowing him, he wouldn't take any money from any sort of publicity anyway.

And, if there's anyone who still isn't convinced, I challenge them to take a good, hard look at their own lives, before commenting on mine.

It's a fair criticism of me to suggest that, if I was suffering so much over all the publicity, I should have said something to Charles. Well, at that time I was in a very vulnerable position, and I did not want to cause any problems. A part of me also believed that what I was doing was helping Charles.

It was around this time that Charles wanted to get me an engagement ring. I had told him many times, 'Look, babe, you don't need to get me a ring. You can get me one when you come out … it's as simple as that.'

But he wouldn't listen to me and he spent his prison savings on an Asian-style gold ring, which he had chosen from an Asian magazine.

I hadn't yet been given the ring when a friend rang me one morning to tell me that there was an article in the *Sunday People* newspaper, saying that I'd told Charles that I didn't like the ring he'd given me because it wasn't expensive enough! I was really shocked and upset. I just couldn't believe how that could have happened, as there were very few people who knew about that ring.

It was nothing but a pure mystery to me. Neither Charles nor I could figure out how on earth the media knew about the ring, and then twisted the story to create total fiction.

Charles told me again to be very careful, because there were many who wanted to stop us getting married.

I intended to get to the bottom of that one day, because it was exactly those sorts of stories that wound me up and upset me. I suppose the irony is that, if Charles had made me a ring out of paper, I would have treasured it, and Charles knew that.

Eventually, Charles wanted to see me so he could put the ring on my finger. I was so excited that day, particularly as Sami had insisted on coming with me as well. She said, 'I have to come with you, Mum, as I have to see this. I want to see my dad putting the ring on my mum's finger. I wouldn't miss it for the world!'

During the visit, he took my hand, looked at me with eyes full of love, and asked me to marry him. I said 'Yes' of course! Then he put the ring on my finger, and we kissed. Sami started to clap really loudly. It was so funny seeing her do that, it made us all laugh, and I can honestly say that that was one of the happiest moments of my life.

Then, the following day, Tracey organised an interview with a paper about our engagement. She said, 'Saira, this is your opportunity to tell people that the lie the *Sunday People* wrote about your ring wasn't true.'

It made sense, and I did the story, but I was really fed up having to put my side of the story every time something false was written about us.

I also remember the photographer for the paper asking me if I would pose for the photo in a short skirt. No bloody way! There was no way I was going to lower myself to that level; I'm an Asian Muslim woman, and I deserve some respect. The photographer apologised and left, and, although I was insulted at the time, I couldn't help thinking, 'Nice try!'

I have always chosen my wardrobe and clothing carefully, as my Muslim roots and values are still so important to me. The fact is, I'm not even a British-Asian woman – I'm just a normal Bangladeshi woman. Of course, I wore nice-looking clothes for Charles when I went to see him, but, wore even then, I wear modern Asian clothes. I hardly ever wear Western clothes, although occasionally I'll wear jeans and a top, and I'm sure Charles wouldn't have wanted me to wear revealing clothing. I was more than happy to let Charles suggest what I should and shouldn't wear, and I certainly didn't see anything wrong with that in a kind, loving relationship. It showed me that he cared about and wanted to protect his wife.

The date of our wedding was set – Friday, 1 June 2001 – and, as the wedding day approached, Charles and I became even closer to one another. He loved me so much that we didn't need to be together physically to experience complete love and affection. Only he could love me like that. When the people in my local community were harassing me, it was Charles who kept me strong by giving me lots of love and emotional support. I didn't expect that from him, especially considering the hardship he'd been through in prison.

A month before the wedding, I phoned my family in Bangladesh and told them all about Charles and me. At first, they didn't know how to react, but, after I spent an hour-and-a-half on the phone to them explaining everything, they understood him a little better. My older brother and my mother were happy for me; the rest of the family took some time to accept the whole thing. But the truth is that, even if my family hadn't accepted Charles, I still would have gone ahead and married him. As I said before, he felt like my only chance of happiness in life, and he was part of Sami's happiness as well. Charles even wrote a nice letter to my mother after this to introduce himself and to say that he would never do anything to hurt me, but that he would always love Sami and me.

I also asked my family in Bangladesh to place the remaining share of our property and land that I was due to inherit in Charles's name as a wedding gift from me. What else could I give him?

Sadly, I fell out with my brother Raj over my wedding gift to Charlie and I don't think we will ever see each other again. It was other things too. He always wanted me to see me married to a Bangladeshi man. When he heard about the wedding gift, he told me that he never wants anything to do with me ever. I was dead for him. That's fine by me. I still have two brothers. I'm sad that I'll never see his children. I always enjoyed speaking to them and I loved them as my own. I wish him well though.

With only a matter of weeks before the wedding day, Charles started a countdown. We were so excited, it was almost unbearable having to wait any longer. Although I was excited about what was to come, my emotions were tinged with sadness because I did not even have one friend left whom I could invite to my wedding day, and my entire family was in Bangladesh. I missed my father terribly as well, knowing that, if he had been alive, he'd have been the first person to congratulate us.

15 LIVING THE DREAM

As the wedding day approached, Tracey organised a television documentary with a television company called LWT. They wanted to make the documentary about me marrying Charles, so part of the filming would be the wedding preparations and then the wedding day itself. I thought that the outline of the documentary seemed very positive, so I agreed to do it.

In the meantime, I bought my wedding dress, which had been chosen by Charles. I had decided to wear a traditional Asian bridal outfit and, despite Charles being English, he knew deep inside that I would like to wear something that I felt comfortable in and that reflected my own cultural heritage. He had chosen a black shirt and trousers, with a gold handkerchief. Sami chose a long skirt and blouse, and she was really looking forward to wearing them on the day.

With only a week left before our big day, it was strange that neither of us was nervous. We both felt as though this was meant to happen, or even that it had happened before, and all we were doing was simply a re-run. They were such wonderful feelings to have, I couldn't believe that I was so happy after so long. I must admit that I felt scared, too – I wasn't used to so much happiness, and I wondered what would happen if everything went wrong. Up to this point, I had become so used to being bitterly disappointed.

I decided to write a letter to Charles's mother, Eira. I knew that she was coming to the wedding, but I wanted to speak to her at least on the phone before the day itself. After all, she was the wonderful lady who was going to be my mother-in-law. Tracey told me that Eira wouldn't like it if she gave me her home address because she was a very private person. I should therefore write the letter and give it to Tracey, and then she would post it for me. So I wrote her a nice letter and posted it to Tracey, allowing her to read it, just in case Tracey was wondering what I'd written. She had been involved in every aspect of Charles's life, after all, and I respected that.

Two days later, I received a phone call from Eira and, to my relief, she was so nice to me. I thought that I was going to be very lucky having a mother-in-law like this wonderful lady. I reassured her that I would never hurt her son. After that, I always called this wonderful lady 'Mum', and always treated her like my own mother. After all, it was her son who is was my happiness. She spoke to Sami as well and, after our chat, we exchanged our phone numbers.

I must admit, before Eira rang me, I was feeling uncomfortable, as the situation brought back some very bad memories. The only mother-in-law I had known at first-hand was the mother-in-law from hell during my first marriage. I couldn't help wondering if Eira would turn out to be similar, and I'd already resolved that there was no way I was going through that again. My worries were completely unfounded, though – she was the best mother-in-law any woman could ever have, and I loved her to bits. I also have an enormous amount of respect for her from one mother to another, as she has had to survive for nearly 30 years with her son being in prison. I don't know how I would have managed in similar circumstances. That wonderful lady must have great strength to deal with that and come out smiling.

The day before the wedding, 30 May, the newspapers phoned me non-stop asking for interviews, with some of them even knocking on my door. It made me feel really uncomfortable, although I wasn't in the least nervous about getting married. It wasn't their fault, really, they were only doing their job and, if I were in their place, I'd probably have done the same.

Charles rang me that evening, and just hearing his voice made me feel better. He thought it would be best if I just went to stay in a hotel or something, and then, in the morning, if Tracey didn't mind, I could go to her house and get ready there. That way, I might get some peace and quiet. He saved my life coming up with that idea! Before he put the phone down, he said, 'Saira, I'm with you, babe, tomorrow will be the best day of my whole life.'

'Same here, babe,' I said.

That night, I went with Sami to stay in a small hotel in Hemel Hempstead, only ten minutes' drive from Tracey's house. Tracey popped over to say that she had set up an interview with GMTV in ten minutes' time as they just wanted a short interview with me the day before the wedding. Straight after that, I had LWT filming as well.

I just looked at Tracey and said, 'You must be joking! This is the night before my wedding … I need some peace, for God's sake!'

Sami was sitting there with me and I could see she was becoming agitated as well.

Tracey remained very calm, saying that the TV people had been badgering her continually, so please, if I didn't mind, could I just agree to it and it would all be over in a couple of hours. She added that they were willing to pay for the hotel room, and that they were already there waiting for me.

Finally, I had some time to myself. Sami and I sat down and talked about the next day. She was so happy and excited that she was going to have an official dad! I had never seen her that happy.

I was so full of anticipation that one minute felt like a day to me. At about 9.30pm Sami fell asleep, so I went to have a shower. As I washed, I looked at my face in the mirror. For the first time, I saw this amazing glow on my face. I felt as though Charles wasn't only in my heart and soul, but he also had become a part of me.

Only Charles knew how close he was to me that night. I was blessed with such heavenly, sacred love. It felt as though it had to be some kind of gift from God. I wondered how Charles was feeling on his own in his cell.

After the shower, I tried to eat some food, but I couldn't eat anything as I was too excited. How could I eat? I was going to marry the man of my dreams the next day. I tried to sleep but couldn't, so, at around midnight, I went and stood by the window. It was a summer night outside, and I couldn't help feeling that the star-filled sky, the gentle breeze, the silvery moonlight and even the flowers in the hotel garden were all celebrating with me. I'd never forget such a wonderful feeling.

While I had all these warm, comforting thoughts flowing around me, I was also missing my father and my family in Bangladesh. I felt a little sad and lonely at the thought that this was the eve of my wedding day, but I didn't even have a friend with me to put some henna painting on my hands. I soon realised that the only friends I wanted with me were true friends, and all those who had neglected me or turned their backs on me were no friends of mine any longer; they had left me when I most needed them. I was already learning to cope without them.

Then I thought of Charles. He was all I needed, him in my heart. He worked like a medicine for me. He had already said to me, 'Saira, you are my drug, I'm addicted to you. You are in my blood … in my brain … there is no other cure for me, Saira, only your love.' Well, the truth was, I didn't think I could survive without him, and I think he realised that, too.

As the day of our wedding dawned, I woke up early, at about 5.30am, and then went to Tracey's house. The plan was for me to go to her house so early that the press wouldn't be able to get hold of me until later. When we arrived at her place, though, some of the press were there already, so I couldn't ignore them completely. As I was walked into Tracey's house, the LWT cameras were waiting to film Sami and me and, as I went into her kitchen to have something to eat, Tracey introduced me to another man standing there with a camera in his hand. I had known about this man for a couple of weeks, and Tracey reminded me that he was a friend of Charles's called Liam, and he would do us a free video of our wedding day. I didn't have any problem with that.

When everybody had finished interviewing Sami and me, I went to an upstairs room to get ready. I walked over to the window and nearly collapsed with shock – Tracey's front garden was packed with television and newspaper reporters! It made me considerably more nervous. I couldn't believe the interest in our wedding.

I started getting ready with Sami helping me as well. Every now and then, the LWT film crew and Liam came in to film me while I was putting on my make-up and jewellery. I had to push them out of the room a few times, but they were OK about that.

Finally, the time came for me to leave the house. I took one look at the reporters gathered in front of the house and said to Sami, 'God help me!'

Sami held my hand and said, 'Don't worry, Mum, I'm here!'

As I stepped out about 20 cameras started to flash all at once. All sorts of questions were fired at me as well, but most of the time I couldn't hear what they were saying as they were all shouting together. As I was just about to get into the car, one reporter asked me how I could marry someone like Charles. I looked at her and replied, 'Why not?'

We eventually got into the car, and closed the door.

Accompanying us on the journey were Tracey, of course, with a couple of other people, and Liam with his video camera. Then behind us was the LWT crew in their car. The rest of the reporters trailed along in our wake all the way to the prison.

As we approached Woodhill, I was overcome with an amazing feeling of closeness to Charles. When we arrived outside the prison gates, I had a massive shock. There must have been about 40 or 50 reporters waiting for me. Sami was a little bit frightened seeing all of them together, but she soon saw the funny side when one particular reporter tripped over and dropped her camera on the floor as she tried to snap the first photo of us. Somehow, we managed to get out of the car and went inside.

On entering the prison, there was a guard waiting for us. Eira was waiting there already and, as soon as I walked in, I went up to her and she hugged Sami and me. I looked at her and thought to myself that I was about to marry this wonderful lady's son. For the first time in a long time, I felt as though my own mother from Bangladesh had hugged me.

After that, we all had to go through the usual security procedures. Sami and I then got a chance to spend some time with Eira, as that was the first time we'd actually met her. We sat in a room to talk for a while, where I took the opportunity to reassure her that I would never ever hurt her son in any way. I held her hand and said, 'I know you don't know me, but I give you my word that I will never ever do anything to hurt your son. If you ever find out that I have hurt him, then I will take any punishment you give me. I'm only here to love him … I'm not capable of hurting another person because I've been hurt most of my life. We may argue from time to time, but I can never hurt him.' Eira just smiled and said she understood.

After that, we got in a car to take us to the unit where Charles and I were to get married. As I got out of the car, Charles's cell was immediately above us, and I could see Charles standing near his window. He was singing 'Happy Birthday' to me! He was accompanied by another inmate called Ray Gilbert, whose cell was next to him. Charles wasn't wearing a shirt for some reason, only trousers. I could see his chest clearly. I shouted up, 'Babe, what are you doing? Aren't you ready yet?'

He looked at me and smiled, and only I knew why he was standing there like that – he knew that I was obsessed with his hairy chest, so he wanted me to see it before the ceremony. Only he could do something like that!

I was then ushered to the room where we were to get married. There were ten guests in there already, all Charles's family and friends, and a large number of prison guards, as the security that day was extra tight, as you can imagine. Surprisingly, the authorities had placed some flowers in the room as well, and there was some Asian instrumental music which Charles and I had chosen playing quietly in the background. It wasn't long before Charles arrived, surrounded by at least eight or ten prison guards. He looked like a king as he walked in! For a moment, it felt like I was in the middle of a wonderful dream, with this beautiful man walking towards me. I found his mind even more attractive than his physical looks, but I did think he was a very good-looking man. He came up to Sami, Eira and me, then he gave us a quick hug, said hello to all the guests, and we sat down.

For the actual moment of marriage itself, we both stood together in front of the registrar. We were then pronounced man and wife. The most memorable moment for both of us was during the wedding ceremony, when Charles held me very close to him. As he held me, I had one of my hands around his waist and the other on his chest. I could actually feel his heartbeat, and I mean every heartbeat. It was heaven!

So many thoughts raced around my head during those perfect moments. There was so much I could have said to Charles at that time, as he had made me the happiest woman on the planet. He made me feel like a complete woman, and eased my pain.

After the ceremony, our Sami surprised both of us by making a little speech. She stood right in front of her dad and said, 'I want to thank you for being my dad ... I've got a dad now.' Charles was so proud of her when she said that.

My new husband then had something to say as well, but he didn't make a speech or anything ordinary like that; he sang 'What a Wonderful World' by Louis Armstrong! I couldn't believe that he'd decided to do that; it was so sweet. When he'd finished, his mum told him that he couldn't sing! Charles's face just dropped, and we all laughed.

Once the official wedding procedures had been completed, the prison had laid on a light buffet for us all. We just mingled with the guests, and I tried to get to know some of Charles's friends. It was the first time I had ever met them. I got on particularly well with two of his oldest friends – Andy Jones and Ray Williams. Apart from my mother-in-law, they were the only people out of all the guests who actually made me feel welcome. I will always be grateful to them for that.

One rather mysterious guest was another friend of Charles's called Eddie. At one point, I looked at him and smiled, but he just looked away. And, while we were all mingling with each other, he chose not to introduce himself to Sami and me. I would have gone up to him to say hello, but I felt quite uncomfortable because he kept avoiding my gaze, so I tried not to take too much notice of him after that.

It was soon time for the photo session. First, Charles and I had some nice close-ups, and then we had some with Sami and Eira. We then had some other photos, but, when the time came for us to cut our wedding cake, the prison officers wouldn't allow us ... because Charles, as a Category A prisoner, wasn't allowed a knife! Can you believe that? How dangerous did they think he would become with a small knife when his mother, wife and daughter were in the same room? He's not crazy! Charles, naturally, was very upset about that later on.

One thing that really makes me sad about the day is what eventually happened over our wedding photographs. In all the prison governor took twenty-one photos of us, and we paid £21 for them. I also received a letter from the prison a few days later saying that they would send me the photos a few weeks after. About three to four weeks after our wedding they arrived, but I had to sign a document saying that I wouldn't use the photos for any publication, nor I would copy them because the photos were Home office copyright.

As soon as Charlie heard about it he became extremely upset. He didn't want the Home Office to hold the copyright. I then knew exactly what I had to do, I contacted my solicitor and told her that I want to take the Home Office to court to get copyright of our wedding photographs. I made a statement to the court that if they did give me permission to use one of the photos in my autobiography, I would give any extra money form their use to any charity of the prison service's choice.

My solicitor Sarah Staines worked very hard on this case for about a year. She even found me a very good barrister as well to fight my case. In January 2004 I finally had a date for the court hearing. I couldn't attend the hearing as I had a hospital appointment that day and my health comes to me first. But Sarah told me that it would only be the technical argument at the judicial review, so I didn't have to be present anyway.

Unfortunately we had lost the case, to be honest with you I wasn't too sad about it. Because I knew deep down that court would support the Home Office in this matter, simply because it is the Home Office's right to protect their copyright. It's as simple as that, even if I didn't agree with them. If I were in their shoes then I suppose would have done the same. I have no regret on that as I've tried my best. But when Charlie found out that we lost the case, he became extremely upset. To begin with he lost his temper with me for not being present at the court hearing, and not having enough media to back my case. I can understand why he was upset, he wasn't the only one, I was disappointed as well. But I explained to him that I had to put my hospital appointment first. As far as the publicity was concern, my solicitor Sarah Staines confirmed Charlie that there was significant amount of press interest when she arrived at the court. Charlie's reaction to this proved to be one of the first sign that there was to be serious trouble ahead.

After the photographs were taken and the cake was removed, most of the guests left, so we could spend some time with Eira and Sami. We stayed in the same room, while all the prison guards moved over to one side so we could have some privacy as a family. We all sat down together, our Sami sitting very close to her dad as usual. It struck me that she used to be a real mummy's girl, but now, to my delight, she was a regular daddy's girl. I thanked God for giving Sami such a loving father.

All in all, we had a good couple of hours together, and then we all had to leave, but I was allowed to come back in the afternoon on my own to have an extra visit.

As we all approached the prison gate on leaving, the same group of reporters was still there. Obviously, they wanted my comments immediately after our marriage. Once I'd stepped through the gate, all of them came running over to me at once and, before I could ask them politely to move out of the way, one of them stepped on the bottom of my wedding dress by mistake and ripped about three inches of material. It was impossible for me to turn round to see the culprit, so I just got into the car as quickly as possible.

I was really upset about my wedding dress, but these things

happen, and there was very little I could do. As it turned out, I'd only given them one answer to all their questions, saying that my husband and I were very happy, and both of us felt 'on top of the world'. There was no way I was going to answer any of the intimate questions I was asked about my relationship. I felt that that showed a marked lack of respect for my position as a married woman, and my background as an Asian woman.

Afterwards, I wanted to spend some time with my in-laws, to get to know them better, as they seemed very nice people.

Then, at around midday, I had a phone call on my mobile. When I answered it, I could hear a man talking in English, but I could tell by his accent that he was Asian. He swore at me, and warned me that, when I came back to Luton, he would burn me alive. I was shocked that someone would be prepared to direct so much evil at me on my wedding day.

I rang Tracey, as by this time she had gone back to her own house. She told me that there was nothing she could do.

I tried my best not to let things get to me, putting the phone call to the back of my mind. Having spent a bit more time with Charles's lovely family, I went to visit him again that afternoon. It was just another normal visit like any other, and I wore my normal clothes, just as he did ... but this time we were husband and wife! Sami stayed with her new nan, Eira, as she wanted to get to know her a bit better.

I arrived at the prison at about 2.00pm. Charles looked at me and said, 'Finally, you are all mine, we are one now ... nobody can ever say any different.'

I just couldn't stop looking at him, thinking to myself, 'This is my husband, the one I love with all my heart and soul.' We then fed each other orange juice by passing it from mouth to mouth, which was something we loved doing during our time together.

Charles then told me not to be upset because he wasn't going to be with me at home on our big day. He also asked me to tell Sami that he would always do his very best to be a good father. He didn't have to say that; he was a great father to Sami already.

All through the visit, he was trying to put on a brave face, so that I didn't see how hard it would be for him when I walked away. But I knew my husband too well by then; I only had to look into his eyes and I could read his mind. Trying to keep his emotions in check, Charles said, 'Saira, I want you to take my wedding shirt, the boxer shorts and trousers with you – I kept them all in a pack – as I want you to wear the shirt tonight when you go to sleep. And could you give the gold handkerchief to our little Sami?'

My eyes nearly filled up when my husband asked that. I didn't let him see my tears, though, because I knew that would have upset him.

After two hours, it was time to go, and he held me really close to him. I didn't want to let him go, but I had to. As I was walking away from the unit, I felt as though I was leaving my heart and soul in that room. I can't possibly explain how hard that was. With each step towards the gate, I looked back to where I could see my husband standing by the window. I felt as though my legs were becoming too heavy for me to walk. I would have done anything to go back and hold him in my arms once more.

Finally, once I reached the gate and couldn't see him any more, a few hot tears ran down my face. It was very hard that day for us to let each other go. Even half a day together would have seemed like heaven to us both, but the prison rules were there to be observed above all else.

It made me wonder about their purpose – prisons are there as a punishment, but they also have a responsibility to offer reform as well. I know Charles hasn't been an angel in the past, but he has been punished to an extreme extent for his crimes. Yet he hasn't received any form of rehabilitation or support to help reduce his prisoner status. I find it absolutely unbelievable, and wonder how the system can justify him becoming a victim of political decisions.

After the visit, I went back to Tracey's house, as that's what she'd planned earlier. In the evening, I had our wedding party at a local pub to go to as well, organised by Dave Courtney, a friend of Charles's, who seemed to be a nice guy. In fact, his fun-filled personality reminded me of my older brother, whom I hadn't seen for years, and that's how I regard Dave since I've got to know him better.

But I really didn't want to attend the party because my husband wasn't going to be with me. Charles had mentioned to me, though, that he thought it would be a good opportunity for me to meet his close friends and family. He also reasoned that, if I went, I'd be with people and be occupied, so I wouldn't be so upset at not being with him on our wedding day. It would also be nice for Sami to meet all the people who cared about both of us. I agreed that he had a point, so I decided to go to the party.

When I got back to Tracey's house, I thought that she was a bit distracted. I assumed that the day's events had worn her out.

However Tracey's behaviour unsettled me – I was missing my own family terribly, I was a little anxious about meeting my new in-laws and I still had LWT and Liam filming my every move! When I was getting ready for the party, the LWT crew came into the room to ask me some more questions about the wedding day, but that was when I lost it; I simply couldn't take any more. I told them I wasn't going to talk to anyone from the media any more, I had had enough, so please could they leave. I must say, I do feel bad about that now, and I did apologise to Paul and Audrey from the crew for being a little bit rude to them both. I also regret appearing rude to some of the reporters that day. I'm not usually impolite, it was simply the enormous pressure I felt that made me react like that. All I wanted was our big day to go well for Charles and me.

I eventually got myself ready, and went downstairs to join

everyone else. They all seemed to be looking forward to the evening enormously, but I, on the other hand, was missing my husband terribly, and so was Sami. We arrived at the party at about 5.30pm, and were met by Dave Courtney who escorted Sami and me inside the pub.

The event was being held in the function room of the pub, and I have to admit feeling a little uncomfortable at first because, being an India Asian woman, I wasn't used to going into pubs. I mean absolutely no disrespect to our friend Dave, who would not have known this, and had done all he could to organise a great evening for us.

I decided to sit at a table with Eira and her sister Eileen because, in a room full of people I didn't know, she was the person I felt closest to. Gradually, one by one, all of Charles's friends came up to me and congratulated us. That night, I realised that my husband had a very wide variety of friends and acquaintances – there was a firefighter and his wife; businessman Joe Pyle and his wife; a pop group; Dave Courtney; the late Lord Longford, who had supported Charles's campaign for many years ... and so the list went on. The mix of guests in that room showed how wrong people can be when they say Charles has only got gangster friends. He has got all sorts of mates, just like anyone else.

As for Joe Pyle, Charles and I absolutely love him; in fact, my husband looks up to him as his father figure. He is always on the end of the phone for me, whenever I need his advice and comfort on any matter. Joe is one of those people who finds a place in your heart without you realising it.

While I was mingling with the guests, I couldn't help longing for Charles to be by my side. But I didn't want a trace of sadness to spoil the party for anyone, so I kept on smiling despite everything. Inside, though, I felt quite sad and lonely.

At about 9.30pm, some reporters disappeared, leaving only LWT and Liam. I was fine with Liam filming, as I knew that he was only making a video film of my big day for our use. It was at around that time that I had planned to do a classical dance performance for Charles, because I knew that a few days later he would view the wedding video shot by Liam. It was Charles's wish for me to perform a classical dance at the party, so how could I say no to that?

I went up to the DJ myself and asked him to sort out my music, but he was less than helpful, telling me that it wasn't possible to play my audio tape of the music because he didn't have a tape player in his music system. I didn't know what to do, so I then asked Tracey if she could come up with a solution.

The time was now 10.30pm, so I decided to go back to the DJ and tell him that he had to sort something out for me. I approached him again and – hey presto! – this time he 'found' the tape player in his music system! With some relief, I rushed off to the ladies' toilet to get changed into my dance outfit.

Just as I was about to perform my dance, that's when I heard Charles's voice! It turned out that he had previously recorded a tape for us all to offer his thanks. Then another message was played that had been specially recorded for Sami and me, and the sentiments struck home right to my heart: 'Saira, I'm here with Sami and you … you are not alone, babe. Thank you for giving me the most wonderful day of my life …' I could hear my husband's voice but I couldn't see him, making me feel very emotional. I tried very hard not to let anyone see my tears, but there were several people, including one reporter, who didn't fail to notice.

Immediately afterwards, I got up and performed my dance; I can honestly say I put my heart and soul into it. When I had finished, I heard Charles's voice on tape again singing me 'Happy Birthday', and he'd even organised a birthday cake for me. Everyone in that room then wished me happy birthday, and I just didn't know what to say. I was so touched that Charles had done all that for me.

Tracey then gave a bouquet of flowers, on Charles's behalf, to my mother-in-law, Charles's cousin and me.

When I got home, I reflected on the day. It had been the happiest day of my life. First, I put Sami to bed, then had a wash. Then I put my husband's shirt on, as he had wanted me to, and I wore his boxer shorts, too. They were a bit big for me, but I tied a knot in them. I lay down on the sofa to sleep, because, since I'd found out that Charles didn't have a bed to sleep on in his cell, I'd decided not to sleep on a bed either.

I thought about Charles, and what he was thinking at that moment, and I remembered something he'd said that morning: 'Saira, I'll be with you 'til you fall asleep.' I had a smile on my face as I remembered that. I couldn't help recalling the events of the morning, when we actually got married, and just how dreamlike and wonderful it had all been. I was finally a happily married woman. Slowly, I drifted into a deep sleep, with my husband filling my heart and soul. I'm sure I smiled even while I slept.

16 TRUTH WILL OUT

The next morning, I awoke to a phone call from Charles, who sounded very happy, and he asked me how Sami and I were feeling. Then he asked me about the party, as he wanted to know everything. After all the reporters and the flashing cameras I felt concerned about what might be reported in the press. But I chose not to say anything to him; he didn't need any petty problems from outside, as he had quite enough to deal with already. All I said was, 'Babe, I need to come and see you.'

After that, I went out to the local newsagent's to get the papers, as I knew that our marriage would be one of the news items. As I walked into the shop, I was confronted with my face covering almost all the front pages! In one paper, the headline was 'MR AND MRS DANGEROUS', while another screamed 'THE MONSTER'S BRIDE'! That was a pleasant way of starting the day, I can tell you. I bought a copy of each of the papers and got out of the shop as fast as I could.

I came home and read through all of them before I sent them to Charles. One particular piece I found very hurtful – Charles's friend Eddie, who had behaved so strangely at the ceremony, was alleged to have said, 'I'm happy for Charlie, but I really don't know what Saira is after ...'

What right did he have to make comments like that, when he hadn't even taken the trouble to say hello to me, or get to know me? Well, I can categorically state, Eddie, you are right, I was after something from Charles – love! I'm not angry with you, I just feel sorry for sad people like you.

None of my husband's other friends are like that, thank goodness. After the wedding day, Eddie never contacted Charles, who then found out for himself what Eddie's attitude towards us had been. Charles then told him to get out of his life for good. I wasn't comfortable with Charles doing that, as I didn't want him to lose a friend because of me, but who needs friends who behave like that?

A few days went by, during which time Charles and I became even closer, and really were just enjoying being married. We planned our future as a family, with Eira and Sami at the top of our list of considerations.

After the wedding Tracey and I didn't seem to get along as well as we had done in the past. I was trying to concentrate on my new life with Charlie and I think Tracey had some trouble adjusting to the change in his life. At any rate we had an argument on the phone and I felt that things had reached the stage where I had to talk to Charlie about the situation.

I rang the prison to see if I could get Charles to phone me. I'd decided that I had to tell him Tracey the situation between me and Tracey. The call went through to a Duty Governor Wolsey, whom I'd met a few times during the arrangements for our wedding day. First, he tried to calm me down, as I had become very upset and kept saying that I only wanted to speak to Charles.

Governor Wolsey, at first, couldn't understand a word I was saying but, after a while, I calmed down a bit. I then asked him politely if he would ask my husband to call me as soon as possible, as I would really appreciate it.

Mr Wolsey said in a very caring voice 'Fine, I'll get your husband to call you ... but, Saira, don't you think he would be upset as well if he hears you upset?'

He did have a point there, I thought, so, after a while, when I'd finally cooled down, I said to him, 'It's all right ... don't tell my husband to phone me. I'll see him at the visit when I'll talk to him. I don't want to upset him ... he doesn't need any outside problems.'

Now, I can't comment on all prison Governors, but Governor Wolsey came across as a genuinely nice person, and that's a heartfelt opinion, and one that Charles would agree with. If it hadn't been for Governor Wolsey, Charles would definitely have been upset at the state I was in. Thanks, Mr Wolsey, you're a decent person in an environment where decent people are few and far between. I'll always remember you and your kind words; they helped enormously.

After I'd come back to my senses, I wondered how I could have been so stupid! My husband was in a maximum-security prison, so why should I add to his problems? I felt really guilty after that. From that day, I always tried to deal with outside problems on my own, as he simply doesn't need the extra pressure. I loved him too much to see him upset or bothered about things. Sure, we discussed and solved problems if we had to, and he was a great listener and source of advice, but I tried my best to keep the pressure on him to a minimum.

I eventually got to see Charles two days later. Again, he could see me from his cell as I approached the visiting unit and, just by looking at my face, he guessed that there was something on my mind. As soon as I walked in, he hugged me very close to him. Then he said, 'As soon as I saw my babe, I could tell there was something wrong ... Come on, tell me all about it.'

I only told him a little about Tracey and how we had fallen out. However I also told him that I didn't want his friendship with Tracey to be damaged. He understood and I felt a lot better.

After that visit, I had hoped that Tracey and I would be able to patch things up. It was tougher than I thought. But I also had to think about our Sami and my marriage now. So I just kept cool and hoped that God would help us to find a way through this.

What does a woman have to do to hold on to her only source of happiness? Well, I knew that I would do anything for the sake of my daughter's happiness and my own, as we were both dependent on Charles for our future wellbeing – and he was dependent on us.

Only two weeks after our wedding, Charles was moved from Woodhill Prison. I think it was a Tuesday night when I received a call from Tracey saying that she'd heard that he had been moved to Wakefield Prison in West Yorkshire, and that the prison officers had assaulted him in the process. My heart thumped in my chest. I wasn't sure what to do at first; obviously, I couldn't post a letter until the following day. I wanted to phone the prison to find out if Charles was all right, but Tracey told me not to phone the prison under any circumstances. She said she was dealing with all that, and she didn't need my help.

I could do very little at home – I just felt worried sick about Charles, and I couldn't eat or sleep that night at all. On the second day, there was still no news; I must have rung Tracey 50 times to see if she'd heard anything, but there was never anything to report. I was becoming progressively more anxious and upset, and didn't know where to go to find out if Charles was all right. Then another day passed with no news.

The next day, Sami became quite upset as well, and wanted me to find out how her dad was. When I saw her crying, I decided to phone the prison to see if they would tell me anything. I found the number from the phone directory, but, when I got through, they weren't much help. The prison guard said that, if I had any enquiries, I should write to the Governor. I was back to square one again.

Then I decided to phone different solicitors' firms to get

Charles's solicitor's number. His name, I knew, was Razi Shah. I must have phoned about 20 firms all over the UK, and, whenever I got through, I said, 'Please, does a solicitor called Razi Shah work there?' Half of them must have thought I was crazy. Up to this point, I didn't know anything about my husband's legal team, what they were doing or where they were. Tracey had never wanted me to get involved with that side of things, as she had always dealt with them in the past, so I was only informed of what was going on whenever Charles discussed things with me, as he knew how much I loved being a part of his life, for better or for worse.

The next day, I received a letter from Charles! God, I was so happy. He told me not to worry about him, that he was fine and a lot happier there than at Woodhill. The only thing was that he was missing Sami and me. He added that he would call me as soon as they let him get access to a phone.

I was so relieved to have that letter. He had included some art as well, and I noticed that there was a particular drawing for me to post to his solicitor, Razi Shah. On the back of the drawing, I saw the solicitor's address and phone number! I couldn't believe it – only a couple of days earlier, I had rung all over the UK to find that very address. My husband must have read my mind!

The next day, I rang Mr Shah and told him that, before I said anything, I needed to know whether it would be kept confidential. He assured me that everything we said would be kept between ourselves, and added that he was glad I'd rung because, for a week or so, he'd been hoping to speak to me as well. I then explained the breakdown in communication between me and Tracey. He was very understanding, and promised me that he would keep me informed directly about Charles's situation.

Not long after this we were dealt another blow when a story about Charlie and me appeared in the *Sunday People* about how he wanted to divorce me. Tracey called me up to tell me and I thought she was joking.

I went to the shop to get the paper. I got back, had a glass of water and … yes, the story was there. It was far from a joke. I read the story again and again, as I couldn't believe my eyes. The allegation was that the *Sunday People* had heard from a friend of Charles's that he wanted a divorce.

For a few moments, I thought this could all be a bad dream and, when I woke up, it would have disappeared. 'This isn't happening to me all over again,' I kept saying. 'This can't be happening to me!' Not another divorce humiliation all over again. I immediately had a flashback to my previous marriage, when Nunu humiliated me with the threat of divorce. I had just wanted to die with shame. My thoughts seemed trapped in this never-ending nightmare, until Sami got up and called for me.

Obviously, I didn't believe the story for a second, as I knew my husband wouldn't insult me like that, not in a million years. And why on earth would he want a divorce when we hadn't even had any arguments? At least, none that I was aware of, unless Charles had argued with me in his sleep!

Of course, over time, we argued, just like any other couple. But we always ended up laughing about it. In fact, I thought Charles was even more adorable when he got a bit annoyed with me. So, in a way, even our little arguments were enjoyable. At times, I even looked forward to arguing with him, as he sounded extra sexy and a little bit funny, too. But if I'd ever have been angry with him, there would have been an earthquake! But, seriously speaking, whenever we have argued, it has put me through hell and back. The way I've always seen it, perhaps it was better that he took it out on me than on prison officers.

To speak quite plainly, my husband stood by me like a rock; he was my pillar of strength. He also had very strong values regarding marriage and relationships, unlike some men who live deceitful, unfaithful lives. I don't understand such people, and wonder how they can find the space for so many lovers in their hearts. I believe you only have one heart, and that there is only room for one special person. I guess I was lucky that Charles had such strong moral values, as they enabled him to speak his mind all the time whether I liked it or not!

From that day, I trained myself not to react to lies sold by people to the media. I had to maintain my sanity and dignity by not allowing them to get to me.

But letting people get away with spreading lies about me and my husband was easier said than done. I thought I'd better talk to Charles about that, so I rang the prison to ask them if they would organise a phone call with him, or pass a message on to him. I even explained the newspaper story that had prompted my request. The prison guard was apparently unable to help me at all.

It was driving me mad not knowing who was responsible for such an evil story. Who could possibly have hated me that much to hurt me like that?

On Sunday evening at about 7.15pm, the phone rang while I was having a bath. Sami picked it up and shouted, 'Mum! It's Dad on the phone!'

I quickly put a towel round me and rushed to the phone. The first thing Charles said was, 'Babe, I'm really sorry if that lie in the paper upset you. Babe, how could I say that I want to divorce you when I practically live my life for you?'

I said I knew that, and that we should forget about the whole thing. Then we actually laughed about it. I said, 'So, babe, when did you send me the divorce papers as I haven't received them yet!'

'Well, I think I put the second-class stamps on them,' he replied.

Although we began to look at it in quite a light-hearted way, I could tell he was also very angry about the story, particularly not knowing who'd been responsible for it. Sami and I had a nice chat with him, and I told him to concentrate only on himself and not to worry about anything. After I'd spoken to him, I felt that I could face anything; just hearing his voice gave me a lot of strength.

The following week, just to hurt me even more, I discovered that somebody had posted a copy of that edition of the *Sunday People* to my mother in Bangladesh. Can you believe that? Who would do something like that? My mother is an old lady and she did not deserve that stress. I phoned my mother and explained the situation to her, and then she understood. Charles also wrote a nice letter to her to explain things as well.

As days went by, the news of our 'divorce' spread like wildfire around the community. Some Asian people around Luton really enjoyed using that to make my life that much more difficult. I only needed to step outside the house and people would bring up the subject and use it to insult me. One Pakistani man laughed at me, saying, 'Now your husband doesn't even want you! Why don't you jump under my car, because your life isn't worth living any more.'

What I really wanted to do was grab him where it hurt most, drag him to his mother and ask her what she'd taught him to produce a vile son like that. But, as usual, I just kept quiet and ignored him. Even now, some people still ask me, 'Oh! Are you the same lady that your husband wanted to divorce?' Sometimes I give them the truth; at other times, I feel like strangling them and saying, 'Don't believe all the shit you read in the papers!' But I managed to learn not to care at all what people said. I only had two priorities in my life – my husband and Sami.

It was tough, married life, but nothing good is ever easy, is it? I had a load of hassle to deal with, but I never thought that I would be married to such a wonderful man; I felt really lucky. Often, I was asked, 'Saira, how can you say you are happy when he is not living with you ... when he isn't there for you?' I always gave them the same answer: if they thought about my culture and background, they'd realise just how silly that question was. Many of our Asian young men and women from England go to get married in Bangladesh, India or Pakistan, and their partners don't always join them immediately. Sometimes, the immigration procedure can take as long as two to three years, if not more. Those people are still capable of having a successful marriage, whether their partners are with them or not. Why couldn't I? It's part and parcel of our culture; I grew up seeing my aunts, cousins and friends getting married to people who lived abroad, and it was perfectly natural at the time.

My relationship with my husband was similar to that. We wrote to each other every single day, we talked on the phone and I went to visit him with Sami. And I looked forward to him coming home. Sure, we missed each other like crazy sometimes, but, for us, just seeing each other and holding hands was more than heaven to us. Our love was very strong, despite all the hurdles and barriers we'd had to overcome.

Charles soon asked me a number of times to get involved with his legal matters, as well as to start controlling the media myself, in addition to other aspects of his life. He said, 'We are married now, babe … it's not anyone else any more, it's you, Sami and me all the way. So you have to be my eyes now.'

When Charles said that, I was so happy. That was how it should be, isn't it, a husband and wife planning their future and doing things together? When Tracey found out about this decision, she wasn't very happy but my husband's mind had been made up already.

Charles was still in Wakefield at this time and was only allowed closed visits, meaning that he would sit behind shatter-proof glass, which would separate him from his visitor. There was no possibility of the slightest human contact physically. Although I wanted to go and see him, he explained that he would never see his loved ones under these circumstances, as we wouldn't even be able to hold hands. It would be particularly painful with Sami there as well, as he wouldn't be able to give her a hug, and that would hurt both of them. 'I love you both too much for that,' he said sadly. 'I'm not letting my little Sami see me like that.' He explained that it was different with friends and others, but wasn't something that he would let Sami, me or his mum go through. When we asked the prison authorities why Charles had to endure these conditions, when he had always been allowed open visits at Woodhill, we were told simply that there were different rules in different prisons.

I understood Charles's point of view, and just hoped that his solicitor would sort it all out. We were missing giving each other's cuddles terribly, but we still had our letters and three ten-minute phone calls a week. And this is supposed to be the twenty-first century! In my letters, I always tried to help him to stay strong, although he is very strong mentally anyway.

At last, something unexpectedly wonderful happened one day, proving that there was a God up there watching over my husband and me. Tracey booked a visit to see Charles one day while he was still in Wakefield. About a week later, I got a call from him in which he said, 'Saira, I have to tell you something about Tracey. She has done something really bad to me; she can't be forgiven for that. I can't tell you on the phone or in letters, but I'll tell you when I see you on your next visit. Don't repeat any of this to Tracey, but do not worry either, babe, everything's fine. Just try to keep a low profile with her.' After I heard that, I wondered what the hell she'd been up to this time.

Another couple of weeks went by, and I was still dying to know what Tracey had done, but Charles wouldn't tell me over the phone. I had to wait another few days, when Charles was moved to another prison called Whitemoor in Cambridgeshire. Apparently, they were rebuilding some units at Wakefield.

My husband immediately sent me a visiting order to go and see him, although I was disappointed to learn that this was going to be a closed visit. This time, though, nothing would stop me seeing Charles. Accompanying me on that trip was another friend of his, John Blake. John is a very well-known publisher, who has handled a few of Charles's previous books. Sometimes you are fortunate, when you meet some people for the first time, to get a really strong feeling that he or she could only be nice, decent and trustworthy. The first time I met John, that was the feeling I got.

On that visit to Whitemoor, I met John at the prison gate, and then we were taken through the security process and eventually arrived in the visiting room. Once there, Charles could finally tell me what Tracey had done to him in Wakefield. According to Charles, during the visit she told him that she was wearing a small camera in her shirt button. All he had to do was to pose in different parts of his cell, so she could show the world how badly he was being treated. So there she was, pressing one of her shirt buttons and saying, 'That's it, Charlie, well done.'

About two days later, my husband phoned her, and she said, 'Good news! Two came out very well, but I'm sitting on them for a while.'

Charles didn't think much of that, but then a day or two later, he started to think that it was all a bit odd. If they'd come out well, why had she said she wanted to sit on them for a while? He felt something wasn't right.

Within a few days, he realised that she'd made the whole camera story up. When he eventually phoned her, she admitted that she'd lied. So there never was a camera at all. She had hoped that Charles wouldn't realise the truth, and made a complete fool out of him in the process. That was the reason Charles had told her to get out of his life.

Charles finished his story by saying, 'I'm sorry, Saira, that she is not with us any more, as I know that you treated her like your sister. But we will be all right, babe. I despise liars, Saira, and Tracey lied to me. One lie is too many, babe … she has to go. She is too dangerous and I don't want her anywhere near you and my Sami.'

'Babe,' I said slowly, looking at Charles and choosing my words carefully, 'now I truly believe that there is a God up there watching over me!'

'Why do you say that?' he asked.

'Well,' I replied, 'I never wanted to tell you this, but she was making every day a living nightmare.' Then I told him some of what I had had to go through, and I actually thanked him for getting her out of our lives. He was shocked to hear how she has been treating me, but he also understood why I hadn't told him all that before, as I didn't want to cause him any problems.

. I tried to comfort him as much as I could through that bullet-proof window during the visit, and I desperately wanted to give him a hug or hold his hand. He had a soft drink in his hand and I had one on my side, and then he suddenly said to me, 'Saira, feed me some drink from your mouth like you used to on the open visits.'

I thought, 'How do I feed Charles some drink?'

'I've got an idea!' he said.

In the middle of the window there were some very small holes, so we could hear each other, rather like in the bank or post office. He said, 'Babe, put your straw through that small hole in the window and blow some drink from your mouth into mine.'

It worked! It must have looked ridiculous, but it meant so much to us. John felt very sad for us, witnessing the conditions on that closed visit. Then, the second time we tried it, we both blew down the straw at the same time and ended up blowing drink all over each other's face. That was really funny!

After half-an-hour, John left us so we could have the second half-hour alone. I felt so helpless being so close to Charles and not being able even to hug him. During that chat, he also told me that he had been placed in a cell next to a prisoner on a dirty protest. Charles had complained to the Governor a few times, but nothing had happened. He couldn't shower when he wanted, and he found it difficult to eat anything. I told Charles off for not telling me all that earlier, and I told him not to worry, because, as soon as I got home, I'd get in touch with the solicitor and the relevant authorities to look into the matter. I knew how traumatic this could be, as even I had noticed the smell from the dirty protest as we were climbing the stairs towards the visiting room.

When I got home, I was really concerned about the conditions Charles was being kept in. I knew that I had to do something. The first thing I did was to phone his solicitor Razi Shah and explain Charles's proximity to the dirty protest. I asked him to do something and fast. I was not going to allow my husband to suffer a moment longer than he had to.

Then, after making some enquiries, I got hold of some useful numbers of organisations who help prisoners. So the next morning I rang a prisoners' advice line and spoke to a really helpful lady called Nancy. After I had explained everything to her, she wrote a really good letter to the Governor at Whitemoor that day to remind him of his responsibilities, and I also wrote to the Governor.

Three days went by, but nothing happened. I had had enough. I thought it was disgusting that this was an issue of basic human rights and the Governor should take action. Another organisation advised me that it was worth asking the media's help, so I had a good think about that suggestion, and came up with an idea.

I decided to go to a reputable newspaper like the *Guardian*, because I knew that papers like that wouldn't pay for the story, but they would cover it with integrity. I looked through all the correspondence I'd had with the media, and I found a *Guardian* reporter's name and number. After listening to everything I said, she wrote a very good story on Charles's condition and, about another week later, the prison actually did something about the dirty protest.

After that, I had a much clearer picture of how hard it was for Charles to survive each day in prison. Any ordinary person wouldn't survive a day, never mind 30 years! Before, I'd always say that, in my eyes, my only hero was my father, but then I was very proud to say that I had got two heroes. My father would have been so proud of Charles if he were alive. It was my strong belief that I found the blessing of my father in Charles. I said this to him one day, and he said, 'Saira, your dad has gone but he left you to me ... I'm here now.' It was very strange, but there were many similarities between my late father and my husband. It was a strange coincidence, but true nevertheless.

One day, as usual, Charles phoned me and, during the course of our conversation, said, 'Saira, phone up that man from the television who did our wedding video in Tracey's house. Ask him when it's going to be televised and when do I get to see a video?'

I said, 'Babe, I think you're getting confused. On our wedding day, there was a man called Liam doing a video all day and night. Tracey told me that he was a friend of yours and he was there to do a free video of my big day.

'No, babe,' Charles said, 'I don't have a friend called Liam! He is from the TV company.'

Well, we were getting more and more confused over that, to the point where I didn't have a clue what was going on and Charles was even more confused than me.

When I put the phone down after Charles's call, I then rang almost every television station I could find to get hold of Liam's number! When I finally tracked him down, I gave him a mouthful. I'll admit, I was really nasty to him. Once I'd calmed down a bit, he explained that he had had a contract with Tracey about the whole thing, and that he hadn't intended to exploit me at all. I couldn't remember being told about that contract and, if Charles hadn't said anything, I would never have found out.

Having had a go at Liam, I realised that he wasn't at fault, and I apologised to him. But I wanted him to confirm everything in writing, and he did. The whole thing had been misunderstanding.

I decided to focus on the future, concentrating solely on Charles's legal affairs. After all, that was where we needed to be focusing our energy to get him released. I started to build a good relationship with our legal team, so I could get to grips with learning how to help Charles. I must admit, I really started to enjoy the role of being a proper wife; I felt as though I was doing something meaningful at last to help my husband.

My relationship with my mother-in-law was going well, too; she had started to grow fond of me, I think, and she gradually realised that I truly loved her son and that I wasn't going anywhere. Even Charles's close friends started to accept me for who I am. Two of them – Andy Jones and Ray Williams – are pure diamonds, and I came to regard them as my own brothers. I thank them from the bottom of my heart for giving me so much support and understanding. Their advice has also been invaluable, and I don't know how to repay them. If angels do exist, then I'm certain that they'd look a lot like Andy and Ray.

It was Ray, actually, who was with me when I experienced some of the worst aspects of the prison system at first hand, both for prisoners and their families. Towards the end of August 2001, I insisted on Charles sending me a visiting order, even though he didn't want to see me in a closed visit. I thought that it might help his case if I went to visit him. Eventually, his visiting order came through, and I booked to go and see him on 30 August with his friend Ray. I'll never forget that date.

As usual, we turned up at the prison and went through the

security check. Then we came to the unit where the visit usually took place. Ray and I were just about to go up the stairs leading to the visiting room, when the officer walking with us asked us to wait for a moment. He took us to a small room and told us to wait there until he had checked something out.

We didn't think much of that but, shortly afterwards, the same officer came back and said we had to go and wait outside the prison because there had been some problems regarding our visit. I got a bit annoyed at that point, and said to him that I would not leave the room until I saw my husband. I added, 'So go and tell your Governor! I booked the visit and I'm here to see my husband and I'm not accepting anything else.' There was no way I was leaving without an explanation. The officer duly left to find the Governor.

I was very upset by then, and Ray was trying to calm me down. I said to him, 'What shall we do now? If we leave, then we won't know what the hell is going on in here.' Ray looked at me, but I didn't even give him the chance to reply. 'Ray,' I said, 'we are not leaving this place until we get a visit!'

'I'm with you, whatever you decide, Saira,' he said. 'I'm not going to leave you alone.'

After half-an-hour, one of the governors – Governor Sydney – entered the room with two officers. 'Give me five minutes and I'll come and see you,' he said, 'once I find out more information.'

He returned 20 minutes later with two prison guards, and four extra security guards wearing dark-blue uniforms. They looked more like firefighters than anything else. Governor Sydney said, 'Look, Mrs Bronson, you were told to leave the prison but you didn't leave.'

'I want an explanation if I can't see my husband,' I replied.

'Charles is not happy with a half-hour visit,' the Governor said. 'He wants a one-hour visit ...'

'He has every right to be upset,' I interrupted, 'because I've got the visiting order and it says clearly that visit is for one hour ...'

Governor Sydney wasn't listening to me at all; he asked me to leave again.

'What are you going to do if I don't leave?' I asked.

'These men will force you to leave the premises.' And, as he said that, the four 'firefighters' moved a little closer to Ray and me.

Two of them were just about to grab hold of my arms, when I said to them, 'Don't even think about touching me! I'm a Muslim Asian woman! Just ask nicely and we will leave!'

Well, we were then escorted all the way to the prison gate by those extra guards, but they didn't touch us once.

As soon as I got out of the prison, I burst into tears in anger. I was worried sick about Charles, and I hadn't been given a full explanation as to why the visit had been cancelled. As soon as we could, we rang the prison to see if Charles was all right and to ask them to let him call me. They said that wasn't possible until a little later, which made me even more worried. So I rang Charles's solicitor and asked him to book a visit and try to find out what was going on, but he didn't have any luck on the phone either.

By then, I was convinced that they had beaten Charles up for some reason. I just felt it, and consequently I stayed awake all night. I couldn't sleep at all, and I felt so anxious that I threw up a few times.

The next morning, I phoned and wrote to the Prisoners' Families Helpline, the Prison Reform Trust, my local MP, the Prisoners' Family Support Group, the Home Office and the Director of High-Security Prisons. I let them all know that the prison wasn't telling me anything about my husband, and therefore I was extremely worried about him and demanded to be told what was going on. Then, at about 3.30pm, Charles rang and we spoke for five minutes. I was so relieved, it was as though I could breathe again.

I asked him what had happened. He explained briefly that he had been happily waiting for our visit and then, when we were half-an-hour late, he got a bit upset and asked the guards where his visitors were. At that point, one of the Governors approached him and said, 'Well, Charles, you know you can't have any visitors when you are upset!' But, of course, by then, he had become upset. In a matter of seconds, about 15 to 20 of the blue-uniformed guards forcibly restrained him.

I had suspected something like that. After that phone call, I didn't hear from Charles for four days – no letters, no phone calls – and I became even more suspicious. Then, on the fifth day, Charles's solicitor went to see him with a barrister, and he received exactly the same treatment as Ray and I had had. When I heard that, I actually thought that Whitemoor Prison had killed Charles. I swear to God, I felt like setting fire to the world! But I also reasoned that, if something like that had happened, I would have sensed it first in my heart. All sorts of crazy things went through my mind and, combined with no sleep and no food for a few days, I was becoming ill.

By then I had got hold of some more useful organisations, who made phone calls on my behalf to find out if Charles was all right. Still we heard nothing. Eventually, I couldn't bear that any more, particularly as not even his solicitor was granted access to see him. So, as a last resort, I rang the police and asked them to help me, as I believed that something serious had happened. They said, though, that they were unable to help me.

That night, after I'd put Sami to bed, I sat down and cried for Charles. At about 10.30pm, I got the *Yellow Pages* out and found the number for the House of Commons. I rang the number, and a lady picked up the phone. I explained everything from start to finish as best I could, although I was still crying hysterically. The lady must have felt sorry for me, but there was little she could do.

She said, 'Look, it's very late now ... nobody is here to help you. Why don't you call me first thing in the morning? In the meantime, if it's any help, remember that your husband is a high-profile prisoner, so I don't think that anybody would think about killing him.'

That eased my concerns a bit, but I was too restless to do anything that night other than pace up and down my bedroom.

The next day, I called the lady back and she put me in touch with another helpful person in the Home Office. He asked me for Charles's prison number, which all inmates had and, within a couple minutes, he had found out from his computer that Charles had been moved to another prison called Frankland in County Durham.

I didn't believe him at first, so I immediately rang Frankland Prison and spoke to the Governor there. Luckily, he seemed to be a decent person as well, and he told me that Charles had arrived there that same morning. He also assured me that Charles was all right and that he was going to call that evening. I swear to God, I felt so relieved! The very first thing I did was eat a plateful of food, as I hadn't been eating very much over that period at all.

Later on that evening, Charles phoned me, and Sami was so happy to hear her dad that she burst into tears! He was thrilled to hear our voices after a few days of sheer hell. He told me that his back was very stiff from when they had restrained him; otherwise he was all right. And they also smashed his glasses to bits, which we sorted out for him as soon as possible. Well, you don't need to go as far as Guantanamo Bay in Cuba to find extreme hardship of prisoners – just look at my husband's past 30 years!

About a week later, he was moved to another prison in Durham. During his nine-month stay there, I only managed to visit him once with Sami, as Charles found it too painful to see us on closed visits. Even if we had taken advantage of the visiting access, we were only allotted two visits a month and they were for half-an-hour each.

Charles told the authorities categorically that he would not allow his wife and daughter to travel all the way from Luton to Durham for only half-an-hour. Charles also refused to call us for seven months, as he was only allowed two ten-minute calls a week. Is that acceptable in the twenty-first century?

But our relationship was far too strong to let that get us down; we became even closer and stronger over that time. Charles's few words echoed in my mind throughout that period – 'Saira, I'm dying for a hug from you and Sami.'

Sami took the enforced separation badly, as she missed her dad. Sometimes, she used to go up her room, cuddle all her teddy bears and cry. It seemed that, over the months, she had become very close to him, so close that, if I ever argued with Charles, Sami would always side with her dad. It was frustrating, but it made me glow with happiness inside, as I knew just how much she loved her dad.

While all that upset and worry was going on in our lives, Charles became a Muslim, and officially took my father's name – Ali Charles Ahmed – even though I believed that our love has nothing to do with any culture or religion. I personally didn't care if he changed his name to Donald Duck or the Pink Panther. It wouldn't have made any difference to me whatsoever, although there might be drawbacks to being called Mrs Duck or Mrs Panther!

In the meantime, I was planning to move out of Luton, as it was becoming impossible to live there with the abuse I got every day from many sectors of the Asian community. And the interesting thing was that I was never abused by any other groups in society, it was almost always from within my own community. It hurt me enormously, as these were the very people who should have understand us best. I can't begin to describe the level of anger I felt when I heard abuse being directed at my little girl and me.

What really upset me were the double-standards these people lived by, when they claimed to be acting in the best interests of Islam and the Qu'ran, and yet they saw fit to treat me and my daughter with contempt. They were actually behaving according to their own man-made cultural and religious principles, which often have little to do with the true religion. Of course, I cannot claim to understand and practise Islam any better or worse than anyone else, but what is undoubtedly true is that these pathetic individuals give Islam a very bad name, and they should be ashamed of that. I would like them to show me where in the Qu'ran it is written that women and children should be treated in such a humiliating way.

If those are the principles others expect me to live by and accept, then I would be very happy to tell them where they can shove their principles. I believe in God and feel connected to Him and His teachings every day of my life. I have my own values and principles, and they will be a part of me until I die.

At night, I often switch off the day-to-day thoughts, and reflect on what has happened to me, how I've managed to get to this point, and how greedy I've had to be to achieve some happiness. All my life, I've been greedy for some love and affection. Even after all the evil and unpleasant experiences I've had, not even once have I ever felt the need to reject men from my life completely – I've generally gone back and asked for the same thing again.

I think of it a little like a beggar coming to your door and asking you for some food or money. What do you do? You might give him something the first time, but what if he comes back again ... and again ... and again? Eventually, you would simply turn him away.

That's how I see myself – as a beggar. I'm the beggar and I knock on destiny's door again and again. I'm only 32 years old but I feel like 80, as I've lived and seen so much. It feels as though there is very little I haven't seen. You name it and I've probably experienced it already – apart from an abundance of pure love. Darkness seems ever more darker. Some nights I have dreams that I'm pregnant, or I could hear a baby crying and, when I go to the room, there is no baby. And when I wake up, I feel really empty. Obviously I've been craving to have another baby for many years. Only a woman can know how powerful this feeling is. One day I'm sure my wish will come true, as I want to leave a little brother or sister for Sami before I grow old and die.

We had been married for a year by then. One year! It was hard to believe sometimes, although some sad people thought it wouldn't last five minutes!

One day, an Asian man asked me in the street, 'Would you want to marry me if you weren't with that Bronson?'

I lost my temper, took my high-heeled shoe off and went to bash him on the head but, sadly, he ran off!

17 VISITING RIGHTS AND WRONGS?

Something my father used to say – 'Sell your blood, but don't sell your soul' – echoed in my mind as I went through what turned out to be the worst public humiliation I've ever had in my life.

Kate Kray, well known as the late Ronnie Kray's ex-wife, used to be a very good friend of Charles's, so, when she started filming for her television series called *Hard Bastards*, she asked Charles if she could feature him, and asked him to encourage me to appear on his behalf. I had spoken to Kate a few times through my husband, as he'd introduced me to her, and she'd always struck me as a very nice lady. I liked her and enjoyed talking to her and her boyfriend Leo from time to time. Regardless of who she'd married in the past, or her connections, I simply liked her as a person and respected her for being my husband's good friend.

I was extremely worried how they were going to portray Charles in the documentary, because the last thing I wanted was for anybody to treat him in a negative way. I explained how I felt to Charles, and he said to me very supportively that I shouldn't do it if it didn't feel right. But I felt that I would be letting him down if I didn't go through with it, as he and Kate were good friends, and I didn't want to let her down, either.

So I agreed to do the documentary after a lot of thinking and chatting with Charles. I just hoped that my mother never found out that I had appeared in a documentary called *Hard Bastards*! Charles then wrote to Kate, asking if they would introduce him as an 'ex-hard-man', as he was a changed man, and all he wanted to do was to come home to his wife and daughter. She said that they would do that, no problem and, just to make sure, I asked for that in writing from Kate's director.

Once the preliminaries were all sorted out, Kate and her director came to have a meeting with me about the programme. I was happy with all the arrangements, as it seemed like an interesting and worthwhile project to me. I was also pleased to meet up with Kate, as she and I got on really well.

The first day of filming was in an art gallery in London owned by an art dealer friend of Charles's called Henry Boxer. That particular day, Henry was holding an art show in the gallery, so the television crew wanted to film me with lots of examples of Charles's artwork, as though I'd taken it along to show to Henry. Charles's art is a very important part of his life, and it's become really important to me, too. The filming went well, and I spent a really enjoyable morning with Kate and the whole crew.

After lunch, we left for Gloucestershire to do some more filming, this time in Andy Jones's museum called Crime Through Time. As I said before, Andy is a very close friend of ours, and we've become almost like brother and sister over time.

The museum is home to all sorts of exhibits about crime and criminals, particularly the Krays and Charles. It had taken us around four hours to get there because of traffic problems, and I was suffering a bit with tiredness and period pains as well, so I was in a bit of a state when we finally arrived.

They had to start filming immediately because of the time restrictions, so there I was, feeling really uncomfortable, and without any real preparation before the camera began to film.

Andy knows that I have a massive amount of respect for him, but, if I am honest, I would have to say that the museum only added to my feeling of discomfort. It was full of exhibits that were disturbing and unpleasant, particularly the collections concerning violence, assault and murder – items such as an electric chair or a reconstruction of an old prison cell were very powerful. Children are not allowed in certain parts of the museum because of the nature of many of the exhibits.

After a quick tour, we ended up in a big room, where there were all sorts of items associated with my husband and the Kray twins. Kate was busy asking me questions about how I felt seeing all those things relating to Charles's past; I guess she was only trying to capture my reactions, but I was happy to answer honestly that I believed my husband's past was his past, and that we all had a past. What was more important was the present and the future, and that it shouldn't be forgotten that Charles was a changed man now. I hadn't changed him, he had changed himself with the extra responsibility of a new wife and daughter.

As we were talking and generally looking at the different displays, I came across something that shocked me quite considerably – I saw a newspaper cutting framed on the wall, saying that Charles had announced that he wanted to sell his brain. As soon as I read that, my eyes just filled up with tears of anger as well as upset. Who would choose to sell a ridiculous, humiliating story like that to the press? Whoever was responsible simply had to be evil, there was no other word for it. Later, I asked Charles about it and he said that it wasn't true, that someone had obviously made it up to grab a bit of media attention. Just how crazy do you have to be to believe that a story like that could possibly help Charles get released from prison? He needed serious media campaigns, not a ridiculous lie that just made him look a fool.

It took me a while to calm down after that, and Kate was keen to get my mind off it as soon as possible. She tried to cheer me up by saying, 'Come on, Saira, don't get upset, let's see if we can find Ronnie's brain somewhere in here!'

As the filming continued, I don't think it went down very well when I chose to disagree with her on some fairly fundamental points.

On one occasion, for example, she started talking about our respective marriages – hers to Ronnie and mine to Charles. She asked me on camera, 'Saira, you are a bit like me, aren't you? Your marriage to Charlie is no different to my marriage to Ronnie. In a way, we are the same.'

I looked at Kate and said, 'Well, no, I think we are two completely different women and there are a lot of differences between my husband and your ex-husband.'

I swear to God, I certainly didn't intend that to be disrespectful in any way, I was simply stating a fact – I thought they were quite different, and I would have said exactly the same thing if Ronnie had been standing right in front of me. And I didn't even know the man; everything I knew about him I'd heard from others, so I wouldn't dream of disrespecting someone I'd never met.

I don't think Kate liked my answer.

The next day, the crew arrived at our house at about 9.30am, with the morning being taken up with interviews with Sami and myself. I found most of the interviewing very difficult to handle. But I couldn't tell Kate that I didn't want to carry on with the filming, as I had had to sign an agreement with them in advance.

In the afternoon, we were to film outside Woodhill Prison, where Charles and I got married. The idea was for Kate and I to chat about the wedding day, so there we were on top of a small hill behind the prison. First, we just chatted generally about the day, but then Kate asked me some deeply personal, and, for me, embarrassing questions.

I then had to perform a piece of classical Indian dance, as I had previously agreed to allow them to film me dancing. They had booked a community hall in Milton Keynes for the purpose, and somehow I got through that session as well and came back home.

On the last day of the filming was the worst. I was supposed to walk Sami to her karate class and they would film us as we went. I wasn't too sure how sensible that would be, as I live right in the middle of the Asian community. So I told Kate's director Toni that I didn't want to invite extra problems by doing that, because most of the local young Asian people weren't in favour of our relationship at all.

Toni said that they weren't going to be too close to us when they were filming Sami and me, in fact, they would be a long way away. I still had misgivings, but I went ahead anyway and started to walk Sami to her lesson. Thank God it was early in the morning, as the local Asian population were still asleep and their shops were all still shut. We were all right until I dropped Sami off at her karate class.

After that, Toni wanted to film on our high street. I objected at first but in the end, I said, 'Go on then ... what the hell! What can be any worse than the situation I'm in already?'

So I ended up walking with Kate in the middle of Bury Park, while the cameraman and crew were some way away from us.

Kate began by asking me why the local Asian community was harassing me. As if on cue a Pakistani man appeared from nowhere and started to shout all manner of abuse at me. I was totally shocked, because I know that people like him harassed me whenever I appeared on the street, but throwing abuse at me in front of the television cameras was the ultimate humiliation.

Anyone who saw that episode of the TV series will have a very clear idea of what I have had to deal with on a daily basis. That was the truth of how I am treated within my own community. After that, I was so angry that I wouldn't dare say what I wanted to do to him.

Shortly after that, Toni followed the bully into a shop and interviewed him!

The last bit of the filming involved Kate and me doing some cooking together in my kitchen, when they would do the last serious interview with me. The cooking part was supposed to be the fun element, but I have to confess the days events had made me very uneasy. There wasn't a great deal for me to enjoy about that last bit of filming, then, and I was still in a bit of pain physically, so the day didn't really get any better.

In addition to all that, I had received some bad news about Charles that day as well. I had had a letter that morning from Charles saying that he couldn't take the pressure from the authorities any more, and wasn't going to play along with their silly mind games over the visits and phone calls. He was still only allowed two ten-minute phone calls and two half-hour closed visits a month. Therefore, he wasn't going to play into their hands, and would not be requesting any visits and phone calls for the time being. That way, he reasoned, they couldn't take away what he didn't have in the first place.

You can imagine how I felt, but I didn't blame him for making that decision; he was the one serving the prison sentence, and he had to serve it in his own way. I felt so upset at not being able to see or hug him, and was worried for him knowing how he must have been feeling. All in all, I felt really helpless.

Despite feeling awful, I carried on with the filming. Later that evening, Kate was going to show me how to make an apple pie, and I was going to cook some traditional Bangladeshi food. But, because of how I was feeling, I just couldn't continue with a light-hearted cooking session. I explained my feelings to Toni and Kate, who said I didn't have to film any more kitchen chat, but they would like me to answer a few more questions. I agreed to that.

Kate continued with a bit more interviewing, and then left my house saying that she was in a hurry to get home. Kate's director Toni stayed behind with the crew to finish off the last bit of the interview. It felt like the last few hours had been more like years, but I was also looking forward to defending myself from that man who'd abused me earlier on in the street. Toni had already said that she would give me the chance to do that.

I don't think that interview came out very well. Overall I found the filming pretty hard going, and personally I wasn't very happy with the portrait they painted of me.

A lot of people thought that my husband would never get to watch television in prison. Well, there is a God up there somewhere looking down on us, because, when the programme was aired on Channel Five, Charles had just been given his first television in eight years! He wasn't happy with the show either, particularly Kate's last statement: 'Saira is a lost soul and, if she wants to soothe an animal in a cage, then let her do that.'

Millions of people watched that programme, and I wonder what they were left thinking.

There is a lot I could say to that man who hurled abuse at me during the filming. He doesn't even know me, yet he felt the need to shout at me in hatred. It's pathetic. I hope he's proud of himself because, thanks to him, other Asian men now feel they have the right to follow his example.

Whatever picture that programme painted of me, I wasn't going to let it get me down. so I tried to stop it all getting to me. The way I saw it, these people viewed our lives as nothing more than an episode of *EastEnders*; who was getting the next divorce? When was that couple going to break up? Who ran off with whom?

Something that bothered me even more than these unknown troublemakers were those who pretended to be friends, and who were then intent on destroying our relationship, because of jealousy. One individual was particularly determined to break Charles and me up, because he was able to exploit Charles before I appeared on the scene, and when I was around, he found it impossible to make capital out of my husband's kindness. Sadly, I had once thought of him as a kind and considerate elder brother; but he revealed his true colours to both of us recently, and now I wouldn't give him the time of day.

18 BREAKING FREE

As the closed visits became more and more of an issue, Charles became progressively fed up with his solicitor Razi Shah, as there didn't seem to be much happening as far as the legal process was concerned regarding his appeal. All he ever wanted was to be able to hug Sami and me. Another month went by with little progress, and Charles soon felt that he'd put up with enough from his solicitor. He decided that he didn't want Razi Shah on his case any more, so he had to go.

I knew that I just couldn't sit back while my husband didn't have a good solicitor, so, without wasting any time, I rang the prisoners' advice line and managed to get hold of a full list of solicitors based all over the UK. Then I started phoning them one by one, and interviewing them. Don't ask me how I managed that, I just did! In one day I spoke to 16 solicitors and, out of 16, 7 of them tried to get rid of me as quickly as possible when they realised who my husband was. Then out of the remaining 9, a few were too busy with other cases to take Charles's case on. Others never even returned my phone calls. I was not very happy, having failed all day to find a decent solicitor to take the case forward. I also found the solicitors' attitudes hard to believe; it seemed ridiculous that I couldn't get one of them to work with us. I think you probably have more of a chance finding a solicitor if you've committed murder or rape, which seems a crazy situation to me.

The next day, however, I actually found a solicitor. When I got her name, Yasmin Aslam, I phoned her immediately, and explained the entire situation. I made everything 100 per cent clear, so she knew exactly what we wanted from her, and what she was taking on. That way, we wouldn't waste each other's time. After a long chat, she said she would represent my husband.

I wrote to Charles, and he was delighted. Before anything else, Yasmin took on the appeal case first, although the issue of Charles's prison conditions remained something to be tackled sooner rather than later. Yasmin thought it best to deal with that as soon as she had got the appeal work under way. This was frustrating for us, but we could do little about it, except hope that Yasmin would sort out all the other issues, such as closed visits, as soon as possible. I was dying to have a big cuddle from Charles, but, if that was not possible, just seeing him would make me feel so much better. Sami was missing him so much that she would end up in tears from time to time.

Eventually, Charles suggested that we should make a one-off trip to Durham and visit him. Although he hated seeing his loved ones in closed visits, he just needed to see us face to face.

A week later, Sami and I went to see him. The visit took place outside his cell door. I was really shocked at seeing his general living conditions; a dog would have been kept in better conditions than that. I tried my best not to let him see my tears, as I knew that would have killed him. We sat down in front of him, and talked through the bars separating us. Sami and I only got to touch his fingers, and Sami sat there holding his fingers through the bars during the entire visit.

Sami took some soft drinks and chocolate for her dad. She broke the chocolate into small bits and fed him as well as me. We weren't even allowed to pass a can of drink to him. The prison guards had to pour it into Charles's mug then pass that under the flap to him. That mug must have been at least ten years old and looked filthy. But, before the guard passed the mug through the flap, I drank a little bit from it. Well, if it was good enough for him ...

That was the last time I saw my babe for a long time. If I'd known that there and then, I would have kissed his shoes through those bars. I wouldn't have cared how many prison guards and cameras were looking at me.

After that visit, Charles was feeling awful about not being able to give our Sami a hug. He said, 'Saira, let's fight for our open visits now, as it's evil of them to put us on closed visits.' So he stopped having visits and phone calls, although we still wrote to each other every single day.

We left the fight for our rights to our solicitor Yasmin, who initially approached the relevant authorities and, if nothing happened there, we decided we would take them to court. Seven months passed like that and, during that time, Yasmin tried every single avenue open to her. I personally wrote to my local MP and the Director of High-Security Prisons, but I didn't get anywhere. Something I've learned out of all this is that the British prison system does nothing to keep families together.

Despite that, those seven months saw us drawing strength from each other, Sami included, and I felt that we became even closer. I reminded Charles that, for 80 per cent of Asian marriages, this would be perfectly normal. As I stated before, there are numerous examples of married couples who cannot see each other for ages for all sorts of reasons, but they still manage to have happy, secure marriages. I told Charles that, if things ever got too much, we should consider ourselves lucky compared to them, as we could see each other twice a month, while they might only get to see their partners once a year. We got our letters every day, while they might have to wait a week to receive a letter from places like Bangladesh. I'm sure this helped Charles a great deal. Something else that helped me personally was finding a couple of people in the prison who were prepared to talk to me and treat me like a responsible adult on the phone. They were able to give me a basic report on how Charles was, whether he was eating all right and so on, and their decency and kindness enabled me to get through those long periods of silence much more bearably. Thanks to them for being decent people.

It was nearly eight months without any visits or phone calls, when, one evening, the phone rang. I was sitting on the sofa relaxing with a cup of tea, and Sami was doing some school work; I picked up the phone and said, 'Hello?' Then I heard Charles's voice.

'Saira, I couldn't wait any longer, babe, I had to call you two up.'

Our Sami was in tears hearing her dad after so long. I was so pleased to hear his voice I just didn't know how to react. I felt as though he'd breathed life into me again. Charles did start to use the phone calls after that, but he still wouldn't accept closed visits.

Regardless of all the hardship we were going through, we were still very happy. My close friends often used to say that I was glowing with love. Within a short time, Charles had given me so much love that I actually felt the glow inside me and surrounding me as well.

In September 2002, Sami was due to start at Denbigh High School in Luton. Before her first day there, she attended an orientation day with the rest of her class ... and it turned out to be her last day as well.

I was a bit worried about Sami starting there, as some of the Denbigh High School children had been harassing both of us whenever they saw us outside. I was also a little more anxious because Sami didn't want me to pick her up from inside the school, she wanted to come home alone, like any other 'grown-up' school kid. So, at about 3.30pm, I was waiting at our gate, looking out for Sami. Soon, I could see her walking very slowly with her head down. I could sense that something had happened at school, as Sami never walked in such a dispirited way normally.

As soon as she got home, she threw her bag on the floor and, with tears in her eyes, she said, 'Mum, I'm not going to that school ever again.'

She was so upset that she couldn't even talk properly. After a while, she explained that about 40 Asian girls surrounded her in the loo, and started verbally abusing her about her dad. Our Sami is a very strong girl, but even she was frightened, particularly when a few of them said they were going to teach her a lesson.

After listening to Sami, I thought to myself that we'd taken enough shit from these bullies. The first thing I did was to inform Sami's teachers at the school, and I reported the matter to the school's education officer as well. Apparently, they were aware of the situation, but were either completely incompetent at handling it, or chose not to bother. It became clear to me that they were either unable or unwilling to help, which does make me wonder what sort of teachers we have teaching in our schools. They couldn't give me a solution to the problem, and I was not satisfied with their pathetic answers; as far as I'm concerned, what is right is right, and what is wrong is wrong – end of story.

I also wondered about these children's parents. I know that the teachers can only do so much if the parents haven't brought their kids up with the right morals and values in the first place. There is a world of difference, I'm glad to say, between our Sami and those children. Sami wouldn't dream of acting with the sort of cruelty displayed by those children from Denbigh High School. And I brought her up, through all our hardships, all by myself from day one. So what does that tell you about their parents?

Sometimes, it seems as though the only rational explanation for that sort of bullying isn't anything to do with culture or religion – it's just a sort of basic malicious desire to make other people's lives hell, as though they've all been infected with some sort of disease.

As I was forced to take the matter into my own hands, I kept Sami at home for a few days. In that time, I thought she might feel less concerned about what had happened and go back to school. When Charles heard about it he was very worried for Sami. After a week, Sami was still refusing to go to school, as she was still clearly frightened. I rang the education officer to see if she had any way of helping Sami, and I even invited her to our home to discuss things, but none of that helped.

Something Sami said to me over that period really hit home: 'Mum, they used to pick on me when I never had a dad, and now they pick on me for having a dad who loves me a lot.'

Although Charles felt really helpless, he tried to help the situation as much as he could by writing a letter to the schoolchildren. He wanted them to know that he had become a Muslim and that he loved the Asian people and their culture. He made it clear that he loved us very much and asked them not to harass our Sami. Charles asked the headteacher to read that letter during assembly, but his request was turned down. The headteacher explained that they didn't read personal letters in assembly, but, by doing that, an opportunity to educate some of the bullies was lost.

Ultimately, there was little point in pursuing any other avenues with Denbigh High School; if the parents, children and teachers were all prepared to let that sort of behaviour occur, and then do nothing about it, they all deserved each other. We decided to leave them to it, and I found another school for Sami about three months later. She had to travel there by bus every morning, but at least she was safe.

In the year since I last visited my husband, we became stronger and even closer. Charles was eventually transferred to Wakefield Prison in West Yorkshire at the end of 2002, which brought sighs of relief all round! His conditions there were slightly better than at Durham Prison, and the visits were semi-open, which meant that we were allowed a degree of touching, but no more. The first thing Charles did was send a visiting order for Sami and myself, as we couldn't wait a second longer than we had to see each other. As far as we were concerned, even just seeing each other and holding hands was more than heaven, and anything else was a bonus.

When we finally got to visit him, there were two chairs for us behind a table which was pushed up against a window with bars in it; on the prisoner's side of the window was another table, with a chair for him. If you sat on the chairs, you physically couldn't touch, so we would have been unable to hold his hands or give him a kiss. So Sami and I both sat on the table, and that way we were able to hold Charles's hands and give him a kiss through the bars. What a joke! Charles was no danger to anyone whatsoever, and yet rapists and killers got open visits. Where's the sense in that?

As my husband's appeal approached, it started to worry us that our solicitor Yasmin Aslam seemed unable to cope with the workload. She was, after all, a trainee solicitor, and it could well have been too big a case for her firm to handle, but, whatever the reasons, we knew that something had to be done or the appeal would fail before it was even heard. At the same time, one of Charles's previous solicitors, Tahir Khan, offered to take on the case, so we let Yasmin go and handed the case to Mr Khan.

After exactly six months, though, he was still unable to complete my husband's case due to some problems getting legal aid. I was amazed, and Charles was devastated as six months of his time had been wasted. He became very depressed, as anybody would have done. So Tahir Khan had to go as well, and we were left with no solicitor and hardly any work completed on his appeal. I started to panic, then, big time.

We needed a solicitor fast. I started phoning around for one, but I had no luck for three days. Then, on the off-chance, I phoned our friend Joe Pyle; I reckoned, as a businessman, he might know a suitable solicitor. I was in luck. Joe put me in touch with a solicitor within half-an-hour, and soon I was speaking to Richard Mallet, the senior partner of Mallet Solicitors, a well-established and well-connected firm. It was exactly what I needed, and I'd soon told him all about the case. I also explained how we had been let down by many solicitors up to that point, and he reassured me that they would do their very best and would try to get my husband the justice he deserves. Richard took on the case and worked very hard for a year to get it ready for the appeal hearing. We were so lucky to find Richard, who even found us a very good barrister and a QC to fight our case.

It had been nearly three years since we got married; our relationship had grown even closer in that time, with Charles and Sami becoming my be-all and end-all. Our hopes for his appeal were dashed earlier in 2004, when three judges from the Court of Appeal deferred the decision on his release to the Parole Board. If the worst comes to the worst, at least he doesn't have too long to serve.

And we were heartened that something good came out of it all. The judges also accepted the fact that my husband had changed since he had been married, and that he now had the responsibility of a wife and daughter. He can be given a fair chance, but the ultimate decision now lies with the Parole Board. This is not the end of his fight, though; we will take this to the European Court of Human Rights if he has to.

At the Appeal Court hearing, none of Charles's witnesses were allowed to give evidence, except me. I was my husband's character witness, and felt really nervous, as I'd never spoken in a court before. It is funny to look back on it now, and remember how I was trying desperately to think of all the 'posh words' to use, so I could make a good impression on the judges. But with nerves, my voice lurched from really loud to almost inaudible, and my knees shook as well. But, as soon as I looked at Charles, who was present in the court as well, it seemed as though nothing was impossible. I spoke the truth and nothing but the truth, and explained how my husband had changed over the four years that we had been together. I never made any excuses for my husband, I just let the truth speak on his behalf.

I never thought that this is how I would end my book. Perhaps I should have remembered that there always seems to be this big dark cloud waiting just around the corner, to surround my life in darkness. Sometimes I feel as if God Himself created me and forgot about me by mistake!

I never thought that I would have to choose between my own sanity and my husband, Charles. We all know that married couples have their share of ups and downs, it's only normal. In fact, arguments and disagreements every now and then can make a relationship stronger. But having arguments is one thing; protecting one's sanity is something else.

The moment I married Charles I took on a huge responsibility and every step of the way I proudly fulfilled that responsibility. Charles, his mother and his closest friends would be the first ones to admit this. I've also known from day one that this wouldn't be a normal relationship, but I've always made sure that my input in this marriage was more than Charles's, because he's in prison. For the last four and half years I have stood by him like a rock. While Charles was being strong in prison, I was the strong one in our relationship and, with God as my witness, I have been very strong.

Truly my strength could have lasted until the day that he came out.

Until very recently I used to think that I couldn't live without my husband, but I'm sorry to say that I was wrong, because I have found I can live without him but not without my dignity. His friends have asked me to reconsider but when I look at the situation, I feel that there is nothing to reconsider.

This is how the entire nightmare started. After Charles lost his appeal, I located a human rights solicitor to see what was the best way to carry on with our fight to release him from prison. We also began a website campaign for him and through a friend Charles organised a launch party in a London pub.

I was pleased that we were fighting for his freedom again after the disappointment of the appeal. Charles wrote to me and told me that I didn't have to go to the party if I didn't want to because it was in a pub. He wasn't going to force me if I didn't want to go; it was entirely my choice. But I wanted to go, it was my husband's campaign party and I should be there. So in advance I arranged to attend with one of our friends called Stuart Cheshire, who is like a brother to me. We decided that on the day of the party Stuart would pick me up and we'd go together.

On 1 September both Charles and I were shocked to hear the terrible news from Russia about the awful massacre at a school in the small Russian town of Beslan. It goes without saying that both Charles and I were utterly horrified by what we saw. Whoever was responsible for those events has nothing to do with any culture that I have ever had anything to do with. Certainly the idea that they were acting as 'good Muslims' is ridiculous to me.

Sadly my husband did not see it that way and, about two weeks before Charles's launch party, I received a shocking letter from him. I was utterly devastated by what he wrote. Of course, he is entitled to his opinion but what he wrote has driven a wedge between Charles and me that I don't think we will ever overcome. From then on, he said, he didn't want me to ever wear any of my 'Muslim' clothes. He had had enough of religion. He felt, as I had been in this country for 14 years, it was time I dressed as a Western woman, and that I should only go to his campaign party wearing Western clothes, otherwise I shouldn't go at all. He said that I made his friends feel uncomfortable whenever they saw me wearing 'Muslim' clothes. He didn't like the fact that I had said I was a Muslim and sworn on the Qu'ran before giving evidence at his appeal in April, and he thought I had let him down by leaving by the back door of the court that day. He finished by asking me not to go and visit him in 'Muslim' clothes.

I felt physically shaken after I read the letter. Immediately I wrote him a nice letter to calm him down. First of all I explained that the clothes that I wear are not 'Muslim' clothes; there is no such thing as 'Muslim' clothes. The kind of clothes I like to wear are called Shalwar-kameez. They are Asian clothes, meaning that women from all over Bangladesh, India and Pakistan wear them. Then I wrote that I didn't understand why he wanted me to change myself, when he had done nothing but praise my clothes in his letters from the day we first met. On our visits together, he used to spend the whole of the first five minutes praising my clothes. I wrote that I was hurt by his letter, and that it had really shocked me. I told him that I didn't want to change myself at all, and, after knowing me for four and half years, why did he want me to change now? I told him, if I went to the party wearing Western clothes, I wouldn't be able to look myself in the mirror again. I felt that way because he married me knowing who I was and, now, he was asking me to change my clothes and way of life and it felt like I would lose my self-respect totally. I believed that, if I listened to him and did exactly what he asked me to do, there wouldn't be any difference between the Saira twelve years ago and the Saira now. I reminded him that he knew from day one that I was born in a Muslim family, so therefore I am a Muslim person. But I am not a practising Muslim, and I am not a religious person; there is a big difference. The reason why I had put my hand on the Qu'ran before speaking at his appeal was because that's the law and I had to do as the court instructed. And, even though he knew this, I had to remind him again why I had to leave the court through the back door. It wasn't because I was trying to avoid the media at the front gate; it was because after he lost his appeal I was extremely upset and for some reason my nose started to bleed. Seeing me like this, his solicitor and barrister decided that I should go through the judge's entrance, and go home and rest. They were going to make a statement later on that day anyway. When I arrived home I organised a live interview with *Sky News* and it was then that I spoke about how he felt after he lost his appeal and how we all felt. Even though he knew all this, I had to repeat it all. I also sent his visiting order back, as I was due to visit him that week. I wasn't going to wear Western clothes as he had told me to wear.

Lastly, I explained to him that, if he ever wanted me to wear any particular Western outfit, and if he asked me nicely, I would have bought the best Western outfit in the town because he was my husband and wanted to see me in that particular outfit. However, this just felt like I was being forced to wear Western clothes and all for the wrong reasons.

I posted the letter to Charles and hoped that he would come to his senses and everything would be all right.

Two days later he replied to my letter by repeating what he wrote in his first letter. I just felt even more hurt. He is entitled to his opinion, but I just couldn't compromise in this situation. To me my dignity and self-respect mean a great deal. Without my dignity I might as well be a dog on the street! I wasn't angry with him at all; I just felt very empty inside for some reason. I didn't want history to repeat itself.

Two weeks passed and I'm sorry to say that his letters continued in the same vein. I wrote back to him and tried to change his mind, but failed. He hasn't even phoned me since then. I decided not to go to his campaign party because, as I said, if I did wear Western clothes, I would never be able to look myself in the mirror again.

Some people might think that I chose my Asian outfit over my husband, but it wasn't a question of that. I had to protect my sanity.

Personally I don't really prefer either Western or Eastern clothes. I think we wear clothes mainly to cover our bodies, wherever we come from. When I was growing up in Bangladesh, whenever we would see Western women wearing our traditional Bangladesh clothes and jewellery, we used to think they looked like princesses. I'd prefer not to use the term 'Western' clothes – they are modern clothes, that's all. In addition to all this I wouldn't really wear a Shalwar-kameez in a pub! I would have worn something East–West mixed. I don't have anything against any clothes; I think it's really nice how the high-street fashion stores mix and match Western and Eastern fabrics.

Also I have never put pressure on Charles to convert to Islam. He did so of his own free will. I have four and a half years of letters to prove this. In fact when we met for the very first time, I said to him that when we live together we won't have a 'Bangladeshi' home or an 'English' home. We'll call it 'our home'. When we had children they would be our children, not English or Bangladeshi children. He agreed one hundred percent. He agreed that we wouldn't let any race, culture or religion come in between us.

While I was trying to calm my husband down and save my marriage, one day one of our friends phoned me and asked me, 'Saira, did you see what Charles put on his website about you?'

I said I hadn't.

He read the whole thing to me. It was a statement written against me by Charles. He had put it all there, starting from when he wanted me to change my clothes for the party and he also expressed his opinion of Muslims and Islam. It was more horrific than I ever would have expected. Later on I read it myself and I felt so hurt that my mind and body became numb.

I was so hurt that, for the first time in the last three and half years, I couldn't walk along the street with my head up high. My husband had been the crown on my head over that last four and half years, and now he wasn't any more. I felt as if I had been stabbed in the back, pushed off a cliff and left in darkness.

It wasn't long before the media got hold of the story and they began writing to me, knocking on my door and calling my house. I'm not angry with them as they were only doing their job. But what could I tell them? What could I do?

In the end I told them I had nothing to say. The next day the *Mirror* and the *Sun* did a story based on what had appeared on Charles's website. Within a day or two it seemed like the whole world knew. There is a small paper in Luton called *Luton on Sunday*. It gets delivered free door to door and they were the worst of all. They published my home address! Can you believe it? As if I hadn't had enough trouble already from my community.

By then, my Sami became aware of the whole situation. She was very upset. She was very close to Charles and I don't think even she ever thought that this would happen. She doesn't even write to him any more. I can see in her eyes how much hurt she feels. The other day she came up to me and said, 'Don't worry, Mum, it's us two again; we'll have to be all right.'

I just comfort her as much as I can. I can tolerate anything but I can't bare to see tears in my Sami's eyes. We both made a promise to each other that I won't cry about it any more and she won't feel sad about it any more. At the moment we are doing our best to stick to our promises. She will be all right, as she is her mummy's daughter.

I must admit I'm very proud of Sami. She has done very well in her karate, she is now a brown belt! I'll always be grateful to her three martial art instructors Leo, Jason and Michael at the Shires Karate Academy. Thanks to all three of them my daughter has really excelled in martial arts. Sami has turned out to be a very strong-minded young lady. She is 13 years old but at times I feel she is the mum in the house and not me! She feels sad at times that she can't see my family in Bangladesh, but she speaks to them on the phone.

I haven't told my old mother in Bangladesh about it. What do I tell her? How do I break something like this to her? Especially after all I've been through. She believed that I was finally happy.

I'm not angry with Charles. But one thing I don't understand is why men always try to change me! My ex-husband Nunu used to hit me for not being covered up from head to toe and my second husband wants me to change my whole identity and become a European woman! Why can't people accept me for what I am?

I think my dead father's soul would be crying today to see Sami and me like this. Sometimes I think perhaps it's better that he's dead than see this.

I'm not even going to try to change myself for Charles. I would never try to change a person. In his case the only thing I ever tried to change is his anger so that he could work towards his release.

In his last letters to me he said he'd only have me in his life if I change myself completely. He even asked me why can't I be like that Asian actress called Sunita in television series called Coronation street? As he likes the way he talks and the way she is, she also wears western clothes, fun loving and out going. I simply couldn't believe when he said that! It's like me saying why can't he be more like Brad Pitt. I would have loved to go out and have fun, but with my husband, not while he is in prison. What sort of wife would I have been. I thought he would appreciate me not going out clubbing and pubbing every Friday night, while he is inside. He tells some of his friends that he still loves me. But after making offensive comments on his website and telling me to change my personality completely, I find this rather patronising. I'm not a doll, I'm a living human being, I breath, I laugh and cry too when I get hurt.

I would have done anything for him, and he knew that very well. After he had lost his appeal we actually talked about having a baby through artificial insemination. We even spoke to his solicitor Richard Charlton about it, as there might be a way of proceeding through the European Court of Human Rights. We were very serious about doing this. Charles and I even spoke to Sami about it and asked her if she would like a little brother or a sister. Obviously she was excited about the idea as well, she used to sit down and make a list of names for the baby! But it's just a broken dream now; it has no meaning now.

But it doesn't matter which way you look at it. He says he hasn't said anything wrong so he won't apologise. Even if he does apologise and if I forgive him, how could I forget that, by writing all the nasty things about me on his website, he publicly humiliated me?

I still struggle to make sense of the change that came over my husband. After three and a half years of marriage it seems he couldn't accept me for who I am. It is difficult to have a relationship at the best of times and I can't say that there was any particular factor that changed my husband. Perhaps it was the influence of television, the isolation he suffered in his cell or just too many years in the system he has fought so hard against. On 5 February 2005 I filed for divorce from Charles.

I'm not going to die because I can't be without him and I don't want to die. I want to live, I want to live to see my Sami grow up.

I want to live to be loved and love. Sami and I are alone again, but we have survived before and we can do it again. I'm not angry or bitter, in fact I'm even more determined to see if there is a real man out there who would truly love and accept my Sami and me as we are. I haven't come this far to give up on life now. My journey goes on ...

If you would like to write to me regarding any issues in my book, I'd love to hear from you.
Please write to:

Saira
PO Box 2398
Luton
Bedfordshire
LU3 1WS

COLD DISTANCE

Drifting back into eternal love
Please don't wake me.
Midnight, can't sleep, once again my soul cries in agony,
Broken into many pieces.
I stand by the window,
A distant sound of music is intoxicating me.
The gentle breeze touches my face; puts a shiver
   through me
Or is it his midnight kiss?
Fragrance of his love, his scent is all round me.
Is it a dream or a vision? Who is he? Why does he
   call me?
He is love; he is last and he is pleasure,
He is the only and one ultimate treasure.
He leaves a smile on my lips and tears in my eyes,
I'm locked in myself, unlock me
I'm not caged in cruel darkness any more.

This can't be a dream, it has to be the most
  beautiful vision.
We are together, alone, only the green field, moonlight,
And sinking night.
He's holding me very close to him,
Almost hidden me inside him, we are one blanket of love.
He touches me softly, kisses me,
No more I fear,
No more I hold back.
Don't want to die before I live,
I want to sleep; please don't wake me.
What is this relation?
Or is it re-coronation?
I'm his slave while he worships me,
My world lies barren without him.
He woke me from death many times,
We are so close, yet worlds apart, why this cold distance?
I can't help but let my feelings flow
As it would be insane to let go.

He smells like holy perfume,
His sensuous smile is to live and die for.
His strength is to protect my vulnerability, not to
  bully me.
The sweetness of his voice whispers to my ears every
  lonely night.
What is this distance-closeness?
Who is he? Why does he call me?

Let's walk together on the path of moonlight again,
Love me unnaturally again.
Help me to rise above again,
While cast aside in humiliation.
Don't let me cry,
Don't let me die.
He turns and looks back with the same pain in his eyes,
As I'm standing in cold rain.
We walk back into sweet dreams again.
But it isn't dream or my imagination, or a vision
   any more,
It is purely love, the eternal love.
This much I've known
Wherever I am, I'll never be alone.
Don't want to die a slow death any longer,
   hold me closer,
No more can I stay stronger.
Died many deaths of betrayals,

No more I can bear this cold distance.

Saira Bronson